Praise for
In the Company of Men

They used to say this is a man's world. Eileen Scully just wrote the definitive book to say you can kiss that sh*t goodbye!

Jeffrey Hayzlett
Primetime TV & Podcast Host, Speaker,
Author, and Part-Time Cowboy

In the Company of Men: How Women Can Succeed in a World Built Without Them is a must-read tackling the visible barriers women face in a patriarchal world. Eileen Scully provides a roadmap for every single one of us who wants to improve our world. It is uplifting and refreshingly blunt. The examples of systemic injustice across industry, policy, and society will help readers understand the challenges, but also demand more from every aspect of our lives. The stories she shares will inspire and incite a new approach to activism and action.

Dr. Shola Mos-Shogbamimu, PhD MBA LLM MA LLB IAQ
New York Attorney and Solicitor of England & Wales
Co-Chair Africa Committee, American Bar Association
Founder & Editor-in-Chief of the Women in Leadership publication

As a woman who spent more than 30 years in the male-dominated world of financial services, I had to learn how to survive by trial and error— mostly error. Eileen's book provides all women with practical and heartfelt examples of how we can rewrite the narrative on building our success from within an organization. It is also a must-read for enlightened male leaders who recognize the value of creating a culture of achievement for all.

Mary Barneby
CEO, Girl Scouts of Connecticut

Erudite, powerful, and astonishingly practical, Scully's invigorating perspective on women in the culture and workplace will change minds and open doors. Scully knows her history, understands her audience, and celebrates everyone's differences while providing her readers with immediately useful ways to shift habits and innovate new ways of thinking.

Gina Barreca, Ph.D.
Distinguished Professor of English Literature, University of Connecticut
Author of They Used to Call Me Snow White, But I Drifted: Women's Strategic Use of Humor *and* It's Not That I'm Bitter, or How I Learned to Stop Worrying About Visible Panty Lines and Conquered the World

Eileen Scully's detailed research is matched only by her authenticity and drive to level the playing field for women. Her no-nonsense argument for equality and objective data cannot be denied. Personal stories make the narrative even more poignant and relatable. For any woman who has worked with men who all went to the same college or came from the same company, these stories will resonate. I have a greater appreciation for my mother's generation that still had the "dress code" enforced upon them. I am more energized to fight for the culture shift Eileen promotes. And after reading this book, you will be too. Luckily, it ends with a list of action items to get you started.

Juli Briskman
Mom, writer, activist, politician, and defender of the First Amendment

I learned something after reading the story about the war planes and how to make them better: that it all depends on your perspective. I'd never heard that before and Eileen makes it a good set up to the book, making me interested in listening to her voice and hearing more. At the end of the book, Eileen provides a valuable and eye-opening list of things that you can do to help make the world a better place. This list could be a book of its own, and I encourage you to skip to the back of the book and read it now.

Steve Garfield
Writer/Photographer/Traveler/Investor/Humorist

As a seasoned black woman in computing and tech, I've faced adversity many times during my career and it was in those times I trusted myself to overcome obstacles so that I was able to contribute to something bigger than myself. These stories from these incredible women are shaping the future that includes all of us whether invited to the table or not. Their stories will uplift you, motivate you, and challenge your thinking and perception of how things are today and how you can effect change and create social impact for a better future.

Rosario Robinson
Senior Director, Women in Tech Evangelist
AnitaB.org

Eileen Scully offers a powerful, contemporary roadmap for women—and men—that is both deeply informative and also very hands-on when it comes to what you can actually do after reading it. The accomplished women who underpin her themes reminded me of the many amazing female role models I have had the privilege to work for—50% of all my bosses so far—and the need for more men to both learn from, be allies with, and help women have fewer gender-based obstacles in their path.

Raju Narisetti
Professor, Columbia University School of Journalism
Former CEO Gizmodo Media Group and Managing Editor,
WSJ Digital/The Washington Post

We live in a time when tremendous lip service is being paid to women's equality...and much of it is just that. Talk but not action. And often ill-informed talk at that. In this context, Scully's book stands out in two ways: first, it is well researched and each of her points cites concrete data and history to back them up; second, the women in each of her chapters give all of us new ways to approach our individual and societal attempts at advocacy by reminding us that any success does not end with us, that each of us has a greater responsibility to build (or break) new paths. As someone who is conscious of his own shortcomings and the need to listen and learn when it comes to supporting women's equality, I found this book insightful, instructional, and also very inspirational.

Adam Quinton

Adjunct Professor, Columbia University School of International and Public Affairs

In the Company of Men is a reminder of our shared history, and showcases inspiring women who each and every day are charting the way forward for gender equity. These stories give me hope. Beyond the individual groundbreaking examples, Eileen illuminates what is required by our leaders to address the systemic barriers that stand in our way of reaching a more equal world where women and girls can thrive.

Kate C. Farrar

Executive Director, Connecticut Women's Education and Legal Fund (CWEALF)

Reading Eileen Scully's book reminded me that the work I do—mentoring and challenging women in technology to always innovate—makes me one of millions of others who are making an impact on the women of the future. We cannot work alone; we must pull together and always encourage each other to find or make a better way. The women in *In the Company of Men* are inspiring, yes, but their strength is in their commitment to changing the future. And we are seeing the impact of that already, in the careers and the choices of the next generation. Scully's book is a powerful instrument for breaking the walls that hold women back.

Bozenna Pasik-Duncan, Ph.D., D.Sc. (Habilitation)
Professor of Mathematics and Courtesy
Professor of AE and EE, University of Kansas,
Founder of IEEE Control Systems Society (CSS) Women in Control (WIC)
Past Global Chair of IEEE Women in Engineering

In the Company of Men is a must-read for both women and men. It is a book about the promise of a better future through a better understanding of our past. Eileen Scully shares compelling stories of how women have blazed a trail in the fields of sports, broadcasting, technology, and entertainment. You'll walk away with practical tips and be inspired to take action.

Stan Phelps
Founder of PurpleGoldfish.com and
author of The Goldfish Series of Books

The combination of remarkable, diverse stories from all walks of life that make up *In the Company of Men* serves to underscore the depth and breadth of challenges facing women in a world that desperately needs to be more equitable. This book is both an unabashed look at the hardships and injustices women face and a hopeful, actionable vision for the path forward.

Rand Fishkin
Cofounder, SparkToro

In the Company of Men is the book we all need to read today. It's long past time to move beyond the gender norms that constrain women's abilities to lead in all types of work environments. The book challenges those norms with compelling stories and facts that help all of us understand how we can accelerate progress toward gender equity.

Gabrielle Fitzgerald
Founder and CEO, Panorama

I applaud Eileen's dedication to making the workplace better for women today and for future generations. The inspiring stories shared in her book shine a light on the challenges women face in male-dominated industries and how together we can overcome these when we use our voices to help each other.

Maggie Chan Jones
Founder and CEO, Tenshey

In the Company of Men reminds us that it's not the stories we've been told that will provide the path forward for our 21st-century workplaces, but the stories that have been rewritten, hidden from plain sight. It is only when we look outside the lines that have been drawn for us that our mindsets will be changed and our ideas about how to define success—and who is considered successful—will be broadened. The women spotlighted in this book are the doers and disruptors, the movers and shakers, the ones who will continue to inspire us for decades (and centuries) to come.

Ruthie Ackerman
Former Deputy Editor at ForbesWomen

Buy this book for its collection of inspiring stories of strong women changing very male-dominated fields. But lend it out as an invitation to the men in your life who are poised to participate in a second historic wave. Because it is the men who grasp the import of these stories and embrace their role as stakeholders in society's next frontier who will help shape the future.

Kat Gordon
Founder and CEO, The 3% Movement

In the Company of Men

In the Company of Men

HOW WOMEN CAN SUCCEED IN A WORLD BUILT WITHOUT THEM

Eileen Scully

PUBLISH
YOUR
PURPOSE
PRESS

Publish Your Purpose Press
141 Weston Street, #155
Hartford, CT, 06141

PUBLISH
YOUR
PURPOSE
PRESS

The opinions expressed by the Author are not necessarily those held by Publish Your Purpose Press.

Ordering Information: Quantity sales and special discounts are available on quantity purchases by corporations, associations, and others. For details, contact the publisher at the address above.

Edited by: Heather B. Habelka
Cover design by: Lisa Knight
Typeset by: Medlar Publishing Solutions Pvt Ltd., India
Author photo by: Luciana Q. McClure

Printed in the United States of America.
ISBN: 978-1-946384-72-0 (paperback)
ISBN: 978-1-946384-73-7 (hardcover)
ISBN: 978-1-946384-71-3 (ebook)

Library of Congress Control Number: 2019905790

First edition, August 2019.

The information contained within this book is strictly for informational purposes. The material may include information, products, or services by third parties. As such, the Author and Publisher do not assume responsibility or liability for any third-party material or opinions. The publisher is not responsible for websites (or their content) that are not owned by the publisher. Readers are advised to do their own due diligence when it comes to making decisions.

Publish Your Purpose Press works with authors, and aspiring authors, who have a story to tell and a brand to build. Do you have a book idea you would like us to consider publishing? Please visit PublishYourPurposePress.com for more information.

Dedication

For Katy, a chuisle mo chroí.
Because everything is and always was for her.

Table of Contents

Foreword

The best place to start is probably by leveling with you.

Unless you happen to be from my native Ireland, you may not be aware that "Ronan" is a very old, very traditional male name. In other words, I'm a guy. Which makes me an unlikely candidate to author the foreword of a book that's expressly about the empowerment of women and the expansion of female opportunity.

Why, you might be asking, would such a book not assign this privileged role to a female writer—someone who could speak from a first-person perspective of the unjust, often unacknowledged, and wholly unnecessary obstacles that society has placed in her path and in the path of every woman in our society?

The apparent incongruity goes deeper still. Because in addition to being a man, I also happen to be a white, heterosexual, cisgendered executive at a large corporation. For a book that frequently and appropriately calls out intersectionalities between gender discrimination and inequities of other forms, my inclusion here might seem to border on the bizarre.

But I know Eileen Scully well enough to understand both the depth of her commitment to gender equity and the sagacity of her approaches to achieving it. She is living the truth embodied in the title of Chimamanda Ngozi Adichie's highly regarded essay, "We Should All Be Feminists."

From the moment I met Eileen at an Irish American Business Awards dinner years ago, it was immediately apparent that she deeply believes that this "All" must ultimately include those of us who have perpetuated or benefited from the unbalanced systems described so powerfully in this book—whether that perpetuation is conscious or unconscious, and whether that benefit is as indirect as a centuries-old social norm or as direct as the interruptions at this morning's staff meeting.

"[A]s long as there will be men who only listen to other men, we need more of you to be advocating with us," Eileen writes in the concluding chapter. It is sad to realize that there are indeed still far too many men who reflexively close themselves off from the perspectives, the insights, the talents, and the contributions of fully half the population. Their lives, their workplaces, and their communities are poorer and less whole as a result.

But let me walk no further into the classic self-imposed male bind of making this "all about us." Because it emphatically is not. Not this world, not this nation—and certainly not this very wise and perceptive book.

In the Company of Men is about women empowering themselves—and other women—to seize the agency and initiative that our society has so tenaciously denied them.

It's about Arlan Hamilton, a lesbian African American who, through her success and persistence, has forced the world to reconsider what a highly successful venture capitalist "looks like."

It's about Alyza Bohbot, who took over her family's Minnesota coffee-roasting company and redefined it as a brand focused on building gender equality in the coffee industry.

And it's about all of the other brave, brilliant women featured in these chapters. But it's not only about them. It's also about the women who read this book—and the wives, partners, mothers, grandmothers, sisters, daughters, and colleagues of anyone (whether female or male) fortunate enough to come across this book in the first place.

It's about the strong women who have succeeded in the company of men and, in doing so, have adopted the role of mentor to me and other men around us on our journey to understanding true equality.

It's about my daughter Charlotte—an active liberal humanitarian whom I've had the privilege of watching grow into an intelligent, beautiful, and caring young woman. As she has grown, I feel I have grown too, learning from her and learning with her. It's about my extraordinary wife Elaine—who succeeded in the business world by being a strong, inclusive role model, and gives to our community and our family every day. And it's about the hardworking, outrageously talented women who make up more than half of my executive team and persist across Verizon.

And you don't have to read too hard between the lines of *In the Company of Men* to see that it's also about all of the girls and young women yet to make their full impact on society—a society that I sincerely hope will welcome their dreams, their gifts, and their priorities in ways it never has before. This book marks another step toward making that more just, more inclusive society possible—for all of us.

Ronan Dunne
Executive VP & Group CEO,
Verizon Consumer

I Love Men

I want you to know that. My career is filled with the wonderful male mentors and clients who have pushed me, promoted me, challenged me, and changed me. I have the best father and brother a girl could hope for, and I've been friends with and dated more than my fair share of extraordinary men over the years.

But the 21st-century workplace has problems. Massive, systemic problems when it comes to women. We are still backing into a workplace built for the single income, male-led household of the 1950s. And that doesn't work for most people anymore. Mostly, women.

During World War II, a team of top statisticians and mathematicians known as the Statistical Research Group assembled at Columbia University to help the Allied war effort solve a number of complex problems through statistical modeling. Among them was Abraham Wald, an Austrian Jew, heralded as the smartest of the team that included the men who would later start the statistics department at Harvard University, and Norbert Weiner, the man credited with creating the field of cybernetics. One of their challenges was to determine the optimal construction of fighter jets, and they did this by studying the bullet holes on the planes that returned. The recommendation was to fortify the areas on the planes that returned with the highest density of holes.

Wald disagreed.

He reasoned that their conclusions were drawn from the exact wrong perspective. These planes returned—battered and barely—but they returned, and their pilots survived. What did that tell the researchers about the planes that never returned and where they had presumably sustained the most damage? Not a thing. Their data set was incomplete and deeply flawed.

They needed to study instead the areas where none of the returning planes showed bullet holes to know where they needed additional armor. Because, presumably, when those areas were hit, those planes did not return.

He was correct. Once they determined that none of the returning planes had bullet holes near their engines, and fortified those areas with armor, more planes returned safely.

Sandi Toksvig, actor, broadcaster, and activist, tells of an anthropology class in which her female professor shared a photo of a deer antler with 28 marks on it. It was widely believed to be the first calendar, invented by a man. Toksvig's astute professor corrected the perspective by asking, what man needs to track time in 28-day increments? But every woman does. And for some reason, for years it was assumed, and never challenged, that the creator of the calendar was male.

We do this every day, when we put forward our observations on why certain people are successful, why some make it and some don't, and to whom we give credit for discoveries, inventions, or ideas. We rarely look at the ones who don't make it back, or never make it into the spaces we inhabit, and where they're taking the allegorical bullets.

Changing this mindset is the only way our corporate and social cultures will transform. This book will ask you to examine more closely the ways in which we define and reward success, how narrowly constructed the path toward success is, and from what assumptions we base our ideas of success.

Because most of our institutions were formed by (predominantly white, straight) men, for (predominantly white, straight) men, they also created the narrative around success for everyone, in ways that are just not accessible for those of us outside that category. The rest of us have had to fight our way into that space, through legislation, persistence, demonstration, and resistance.

In 1776, Abigail Adams implored her husband, John Adams, to "remember the ladies" when writing the laws for a new nation during the Continental Congress. His response? Loosely interpreted, he tells her no, but everyone knows that women are really the ones in charge anyway.[1]

Hardly.

The United States Constitution, which John Adams crafted along with the other delegates from the Constitutional Congress, does not contain anywhere the word "woman." Nor do any of the ratified amendments that have been made in the years since. Not even the 19th Amendment, the one that gave white women the right to vote. I was not aware of this until I listened to an interview with Heidi Schreck, author and playwright of *What the Constitution Means to Me*, her 2019 Broadway play about her success as a high school debater, her detailed knowledge of the Constitution and all of its amendments, and her increasing awareness of how it relates to her as a woman.

---

[1] Adams.

so many roots to the tree of anger
—*Audre Lorde*, Who Said It Was Simple

When I founded my consulting firm, The Rising Tides, my goal was to improve the workplace for everyone. A big part of what I do is help organizations bring women into more positions of power and influence by identifying and removing the barriers that exist within every organization. Women belong in every room where decisions are made—without exception. I challenge existing workplace models to adapt into a new order, one where everyone can thrive and contribute at their highest, best level. And it's very possible, and very real. But it's still out of reach for many of us.

My goal for writing this book is to shine a bright light on some of the women who are proving that we can not only succeed, but positively change the world that was built without us to work for all of us. They're doing it by changing the rules, changing the laws, building the systems and the workplaces that we need to all be successful.

I've chosen to focus on incredible women in a variety of industries who challenged existing workplace models and have built ways to make that path wider for the women and everyone else who will follow them.

I've deliberately chosen not to focus on sexual assault and harassment, although I do mention elements of each as they impact each chapter subject and story. As we are still in the nascent awareness, acceptance, and adjustment phase of the #MeToo and #TimesUp movements, I want instead to highlight the other, less obvious but pervasive aspects of the workplace and the world that hold women back. Do not misunderstand—I am by no means minimizing my own disgust with workplace sexual harassment, my commitment to eliminating it, and flipping—or at the very least, evening out—the power dynamic between the genders. This book simply is not the vehicle for those stories.

The lists we see every International Women's Day of the First Woman This and the First Woman That are great. But we need more women to break the existing systems and open up the space for other women and underrepresented people. To make it easier, smoother, less remarkable when other women follow. So, we can stop talking about the First and talk about all of us. All of us succeeding, contributing, learning, failing, growing in a space into which we can bring our authentic selves.

I hope you're inspired and challenged by these stories. These are real women, women who walk among us, who work beside us, who are doing the hard work of changing the world in the spaces they each inhabit. Their stories should be known, studied, and shared.

We need to learn from them how to widen the lanes, while also smashing the ceilings.

And no, by no means is this book exhaustive. Each story I researched led me to more stories that have not been told, more women who have been forgotten, more contributions that changed the way we work and live. I know there are more being written every day.

The most important thing you can do after—or while—reading this book, is to find these women, follow them, and fund them. And find, follow, and fund others like them. We are not all born to be creators, but we can support those who are.

You can find links to the public social media feeds and websites for each of the featured women on inthecompanyofmenbook.com.

Sometimes, You Step in Shit

Growing up, I was the youngest and the only girl on my suburban street. The only language and behaviors I knew were those of the other gender. I met my first female friends and peers when I went to kindergarten.

Perhaps because of this, the dynamics among women have always fascinated me. When I entered the world of work, I became acutely aware of the ways in which women interacted.

I left college after becoming unexpectedly pregnant and deciding to become a single parent at 19. Entering the workforce was intimidating. I felt unworthy, inadequate, uneducated, and grateful to anyone who might employ me.

My first job required few hard skills and I was hired mainly because I got on well with the hiring manager. Almost 30 years later, she is still a dear friend. But the male owner was domineering and cruel, often leaving me shaking and in tears for the slightest fixable mistake. The women in that office were kind and protective of each other, whispering daily warnings against the variable list of things that might trigger his anger. His moods and demands were always hanging over all of us. Looking back, we were a small office, but the number of nervous breakdowns, migraines, miscarriages, meltdowns, and people just walking out, never to be seen or heard from again, was higher than any other office I've worked in since. Since it was my first job, I thought it was normal. But I still could not get out of there fast enough.

I soon landed at another small family firm, but this was entirely different. The woman who hired me was strong, accomplished, and the first to really advocate for my success in a material way—my salary. She encouraged me to take initiative and risks. She respected my ideas, put me on projects that stretched my skills and my confidence, and paid me what I thought was crazy money, even though it was probably what I was worth at that time. The family who ran this company was generous and smart and shared the profits widely with everyone. Everyone contributed, everyone was respected, and everyone benefitted. It was a dramatic shift from my first job. And it's worth noting that, in 1992, the woman who hired me did not ask me what I was paid, but what I wanted to make. I doubled my salary within one year, and finally felt as though I was valued.

What a remarkable career transition for me. I stayed with that company, which through a fortuitous acquisition became part of a much larger company, for a total of 12 years. During that time, we grew from a firm with revenues of less than $20 million to being part of a $300-million firm at acquisition, to a greater than $1-billion firm, the behemoth in our market segment, when I left. Rapid growth coupled with dynamic market conditions felt at times like riding a rocket, but I was eager to learn, and the culture was one that encouraged innovation and experimentation. My colleagues were some of the smartest people in the technology field and mostly willing to mentor a younger, less experienced apprentice. The company was run almost exclusively by white men, but I rarely felt left behind due to my gender. The biggest obstacle I faced was not having my college degree, a prerequisite for many higher paying jobs.

Women are more often made to feel that they aren't grateful enough for the opportunities they are given. That they should feel lucky to be where they are, that there are others who would gladly take their place. I know I was extremely fortunate to have landed where I did, and to work among visionary people every day, quite literally among those to whom the top leaders in business turned for sage advice. I worked hard, soaked up everything I could, asked millions of questions, and tried my best to keep pace. The right people took chances on me—a college dropout single mother—and I never wanted them to regret that. But I was exhausted, trying to keep everything together every day.

Impostor syndrome, the feeling that it's inevitable you'll be outed as a "fraud," is much more prevalent with women than men in the workplace. We fear that our inadequacies will become known, that we truly don't deserve to be where we are, that we haven't worked hard enough or done the research or paid the same dues, or that everyone else knows something we don't. In 1978, psychologists, Pauline Clance and Suzanne Imes described impostor syndrome as "a feeling of phoniness in people who believe that they are not intelligent, capable, or creative despite evidence of high achievement."[2]

Studies show impostor syndrome as more prevalent in professional women, but posit that finding could be because men are more reticent to admit to feeling inadequate. Coupled with a recent study by Hewlett-Packard (HP) that revealed men applied for jobs they weren't qualified for at a much higher rate than women, it seems obvious that women are conditioned differently to assess our strengths, accomplishments, and

---

[2]Clance and Imes.

value in the workplace. The Hewlett-Packard study reported that men will apply for a job when their skills are a 60 percent match to the posted requirements, but women don't tend to apply unless their skills are at or above 95 percent. It could also be a symptom of being first, or not seeing others like you at the same levels of achievement. When you are doing something unprecedented or creating something new, impostor syndrome is a fairly logical response.

This is why many women tend to seek places where they feel more at ease and why too many women leave the science and technical fields early in their careers.

Things were going really well. I had a job I liked with a company that was growing. I liked the people I was working with and for. And I was making really good money for the first time. But I knew that if this trajectory was going to continue, and if I was going to truly move from a job into a career, it would require pushing myself out of my comfort zone. And that required the sponsorship and cooperation from a number of people in positions of power. It was a huge stretch for me, but since I had worked with and around the hiring team, they knew me, trusted me, and took a chance on me. They promoted me into a role with much more visibility, responsibility, and prestige. I was thrilled. And grateful. And scared to death. It's worth mentioning that the final approval for my transfer into this role sat with the woman who ran our global team, one of the few women in our firm at that level at the time.

Our clients paid a lot of money for our expertise. Because of this, my feelings of impostor syndrome were paralyzing at times, even though I knew my team and my management strongly supported me. I was certain that my company would never have hired me were it not for the acquisition because, on paper, I was not at all qualified for the job I now held. I had, as my father liked to say when we got surreptitiously lucky, stepped in shit.

I learned how to dodge the "where did you go to school" question by naming the school where I had attended a single semester, then pivoting the conversation to something else. In that job, it was so often assumed that I not only had an undergraduate degree, but also an MBA, and I would panic whenever I thought I'd have to address it. I didn't want clients to feel that they weren't assigned the top talent, didn't want them demanding someone more qualified on their account, and didn't want to be seen as a fraud.

That never happened. Instead, my clients liked working with me, even sometimes requesting that I be assigned to their projects, and I started to see myself the way they did, as someone smart, who worked with them to bring value and insight into their organizations. But I also realized that the people in those rooms were mostly a lot like me: smart enough, nice enough, trying to do a good job every day, and hoping to learn something new that would make their lives easier. No one cared about where I went to school or how many degrees I had, as long as I shared with them something valuable that they couldn't get anywhere else, made their jobs easier, and made them look smarter. That epiphany was perhaps the most important of my career. After that, I stopped feeling intimidated, I stopped feeling like an impostor, and I stopped feeling like I had to always be perfect.

My confidence was growing, my credentials were strong, and, for the first time, I felt like I was a true peer to many of the men on my team. Along the way, there had been times I'd been propositioned, asked out, or been the butt of a joke, but I brushed those off because they never had any material impact on my career trajectory. And honestly, the guys who tried held no power anyway. For the most part, the men I worked with were respectful, helpful, and harmless, and I thought I was pretty skilled at detecting the difference—until one day when I stepped out for lunch.

While I was out, I was in a car accident. I wasn't hurt, but my car had to be towed away. The cop at the scene was kind enough to drive me back to my office. I thanked him as I climbed out of the back of his squad car and walked into the building. One of the male VPs saw this and, as I entered the building, I heard him yell out from a conference room into an open office landscape:

"What did they get you for? Prostitution?"

Then laughter. From the desks around me, from the conference room, from everywhere.

The impact on me was immediate. I felt small. I felt that everything I had worked for had been erased. I felt powerless. Stupid. They went on with their day, but I was mortified, asking myself what had I done to elicit that response. I never did anything about it, feeling like there wasn't anything I could do because people made comments like that all the time, and I was sometimes even one of the ones laughing. But no one in that room with him did anything about it either.

I had worked so hard to prove so much, but ultimately, I was still just a slut.

He could have said shoplifting instead of prostitution, and I would have laughed too, and forgotten all about it. But he didn't. Whether he intentionally brought my sexuality into it or not isn't as important as his inability to self-edit out of respect for me, or anyone else that day. Everyone on the floor knew I was a single mother, and I was probably the only one on the team, so leveling that against me, in that way, was horrifying. I wanted so badly for that never to be how I was known, never wanted anyone to judge my choices, never wanted to be pitied or favored because of it, never wanted it to be a marker. And even though he didn't expressly say that, it was there. I wanted to crawl under my desk.

He continued working there for years, and I'm certain I was not the only woman who was subjected to his thoughtless comments, some of which were definitely worse. Filing a sexual harassment claim back then was certain to put a target on your back, make you the subject of derision, and imply that you were going for the money grab. Was this even sexual harassment? One stupid comment?

That moment changed everything for me. It proved that no matter how hard you worked, how well you did your job, there were some men who would never see past your sex. And past their own sexualization of you.

After that, I began to pay closer attention to the way the world worked for women and how differently it worked for men. The guys who got the promotions because they played poker with the boss instead of going home to their wives. The ones who were cherry-picked for rapid ascension into management while their female peers stalled out in the middle, never understanding that their fealty to this organization was never going to be rewarded in the same way, ever.

The year I was laid off, 2005, I applied to speak at a women's conference—this was the first time I considered presenting my own ideas, my own data, and not those of another firm or brand. It was hosted by an online women's group of which I was a member, and it centered on women in technology. So, I knew the issues and I knew the audience. My speaker proposal was accepted, so off I went to join a few hundred other women on Lake Geneva, Wisconsin, for a long weekend.

My talk reflected on my own experiences working with other women and those I had observed over the years. How at the time, many women were not strongly advocating for each other. I wanted to challenge the audience to consider the ways we speak about each other and the ways we speak about men, particularly those with ambition. This was 2005—Martha Stewart was probably going to jail for insider trading, Hillary Clinton was running for a senate seat in New York, and Carly Fiorina was getting shoved out of her job as CEO of Hewlett-Packard.

I opened with, "I'm going to say three names, all of which you know. And I want you to shout out to me the first words that come to mind when you hear them. Ready?

"HILLARY. MARTHA. CARLY."

Of course, you can imagine what I heard back. You may even be thinking those words now. But it was my next line that stopped them cold.

"Now, if you will, shout back to me the male equivalent of those words."

Because there aren't any. Most of the derogatory terms we use for women have no true male equivalent in tone, derision, and disgust. And each of these women were incredibly independently accomplished and successful. Was that the reason for the searing invective?

I talked about how women can and should be better advocates for each other in the workplace. How—if any of us are to succeed in those spaces—we need to step up and support the women at whom the others sling arrows. How we should challenge the narrative assigned to successful women as cutthroat, cold, emasculating, manipulative. How even if that might be true of some women, we should look beyond it and respect their drive and achievement. Some women left the room during my talk. But the ones who stayed, the ones who queued up to speak with me afterward, told me that they had never heard someone address this topic—that it was necessary and that it was time. They told me about their experiences in the workplace with women who either ignored them or pitted them against each other.

That experience was the first day I started thinking seriously about if I could shift my career toward improving workplaces for women. But even just 12 years ago, the message would not have been as widely received. Organizations were addressing, anemically, sexual harassment. Some were considering putting more women on their boards of directors. Some wanted broader representation of a more diverse workforce. But none of it had any real focus or traction. And I never forgot that day and the way those women responded to my message.

It took me 12 years to officially take the leap into entrepreneurship, but in July of 2015, I founded my consulting company, The Rising Tides. Since then, I've spoken with thousands of people at events on three continents and delivered projects to some of the top companies in the world. I just may have stepped in shit again.

Like cast-off nosegays picked up on the road

—*Elizabeth Barrett Browning*, Aurora Leigh

My mother graduated from college in 1963 and married my father the following month. She wanted nothing more than to be the best wife and mother when she married my father, and she more than succeeded at both of those goals. But she has a keen mind for math (we do not have this in common, alas) and she could have been a titan in business, had that path been available to her. A natural problem-solver, infinitely curious, and tirelessly hard working, she could have achieved success as an executive across a number of fields.

Instead, she became a teacher. An acceptable path for a bright woman, and one that would support her when she began her family.

Many women of her generation stopped working, or worked only part time, to raise families. The option to work full time and have children was not always available to my mother and her peers, or the women who preceded them. Until 1978, it was legal to fire a woman who became pregnant.

When we talk about a gender wage gap, it's predicated on the value we place on business success and not on those who teach and take care of our families and children. As Anne-Marie Slaughter, noted author and former foreign policy analyst with the US Department of State, famously says, "If we valued breadwinning and caregiving equally, then we would value male caregivers as much as we have come to value female breadwinners."[3] Even in nursing, a caregiving field in which women outnumber men by 10:1, there is a $5,000 pay gap favoring men.

Some of the biggest hurdles for the early female entrants into corporate America were basic. Humorous to us now, but legitimate hurdles and ones not often anticipated by the first women to enter the spaces held traditionally by men.

Dress codes have always been troublesome for women. In the early '90s I worked for a man who did not allow women to wear pants to the office. It was only after J. Edgar Hoover died in 1972 that women at the FBI were allowed to wear pants, as he allegedly "hated seeing women in them."[4] Also in 1972, Pat Nixon became the first First Lady to be photographed wearing pants. Women on the Senate floor were not allowed to wear pants until 1993, when Carol Moseley Braun, the junior senator from Illinois, inadvertently broke the unwritten rule and wore pants on a snowy day. It was only when other women thanked her that she realized what she had done. Soon after, Maryland senator Barbara Mikulski confirmed with

---

[3]Slaughter.
[4]Sears.

President Pro Tempore of the Senate Robert Byrd that pants on women were not expressly written into the Senate dress code rules, at which point she began wearing them too.[5]

The passage of Title IX in 1972, which prohibited federally funded schools from gender-based inequity, among other provisions, stated that girls in public schools could not be forced to wear dresses. Schools still police women's clothing choices in the name of safety and modesty, while saying nothing to the boys about their behaviors and responses to women. The assistant principal in my Catholic high school was notoriously strict about our plaid pleated hemlines, yet the cheerleaders' skirts barely covered their backsides. There clearly was a time and place for girls to be sexual, and those contradictions are still prevalent today.

In March of 2019, a federal judge ruled unconstitutional a rule by a North Carolina school requiring girls to wear skirts or skorts, while boys were free to wear shorts or pants. It started as a petition raised by some of the girls, but the American Civil Liberties Union (ACLU) filed a suit in 2016 on their behalf. The judge ruled that forcing girls to wear skirts placed an undue burden on them, one not borne by the boys.

Debates over women's and girls' clothing choices are rooted in morality, or the attempt to protect such. Girls are told their clothes are distracting to the boys, without discussing with the boys what respect and boundaries the girls deserve. Fox News famously assigns its female hosts a very specific dress code—sleeveless dresses, short skirts, high heels, heavy makeup. Women who work for them, and many other news organizations, are decorative, scripted, interchangeable, and replaceable.

During the 2016 presidential election, Hillary Clinton's pantsuits drew as much attention as her running mate. I'll predict many

---

[5]Ibid.

of us will remember them and their prominence long past the point at which we struggle to recall Senator Tim Kaine's role in the race. The private Facebook group Pantsuit Nation exploded during the last months of the election to over four million members, becoming a place for sharing frustrations and actions regarding the sexism exposed during her campaign. Many women wore pantsuits to the polls in solidarity with their candidate.

Women's clothing often does not include pockets. Many women carry purses to accommodate their wallet, keys, phone, and other necessities. But purses are cumbersome and awkward in a workplace setting. Pockets are most often left off of women's clothes due to fashion, fit, and fabric drape, decisions often made by the men in fashion. Most women would prefer the functionality of wider, larger pockets.

The Rational Dress Society was founded in London in the late 19th century to protest against overly restrictive, uncomfortable clothing for women. They sought clothing that allowed freedom of movement; that was free from restrictions; that combined form, function, beauty, and convenience. Around the same time, cycling rose in popularity, but women were dying because their skirts were getting tangled in the machinery, although some critics thought women were incapable riders and should be kept off bicycles. The freedom bicycles provided women clouded any assessment of the hazards their clothing posed.[6] Cycling for these women, who still did not have the right to vote, became a powerful expression of independence, and they wanted clothing that would not endanger their lives. Quite the radical movement at the time. But these women riding bicycles in bloomers—modified split skirts—eventually led to the acceptance of women wearing pants in everyday life.

---

[6]Jungnickel.

Flight attendants on Cathay Pacific, one of Asia's largest airlines, just won the right to wear pants in early 2018, after 72 years of a strict skirts-only uniform for women and four years since the original request for consideration by the union. It could take a few more years to be widely adopted, as it will have to wait for the next uniform upgrade. Few Asian airlines include pants in their uniform choices for women, and one airline, based in Vietnam, includes a bikini in their uniform, runs promotional flights with all-bikini crews, and sells calendars of their female flight attendants in bikinis. (It's worth noting that their CEO is Vietnam's first female billionaire.) And, before you think it's a regional or cultural issue, it was just 2016 when British Airlines allowed women on their crews to wear pants.

Clumsy but serviceable, that canoe!
—*Carolyn Kizer*, "Semele Recycled"

Childcare has been and remains a massive hurdle for women in the workplace. A later chapter in this book will detail this, but as a nation, the United States still does not provide adequate, affordable, accessible childcare to our working mothers. If we want to provide workplaces that equally support all genders, quality, reliable, local, and affordable childcare is essential. In the United States, approximately 90 percent of people become parents at some point in their career. Between 20 to 35 percent of mothers do not return to work at their previous employer.

Lactation rooms—private dedicated spaces for nursing mothers to express breast milk when they are not home—are a recent but essential accommodation in workplaces. Having a space that is not a restroom or broom closet is a reasonable but often overlooked adaptation. Employment law has only recently caught up to include break time for nursing mothers who are paid hourly and have set, scheduled breaks.

Access to education has also been problematic for women. Susan B. Anthony was advocating for co-education as early as 1859, on the basis that there were no differences between the minds of men and women. She wanted all public schools to provide education to anyone, including former slaves and their children.[7]

In the 1890s, Anthony raised $50,000 in pledges to ensure the admittance of women to the University of Rochester. In a last-minute effort to meet the deadline, she put up the cash value of her life insurance policy. The University was forced to make good on its promise, and women were admitted for the first time in 1900.

University co-education was not mainstream until the mid-1960s. This is significant inasmuch as the alumni networks, secret societies, campus recruitment, and prestigious clubs were shut off to women, stunting their career opportunities. In the late 1960s, more women were accepted into the Ivy League, but they were there mainly to retain the top-tier men, most of whom preferred a co-educational experience over a single-sex one.

Even though the women took their education seriously, the administrations did not. They were seen as taking the spots from talented men, men who would apply their education to the business world. It was assumed the women were only there to marry up or, if they graduated, would soon abandon their careers for motherhood.

---

[7] The National Susan B. Anthony Museum & House.

Once women were admitted to men's universities, they were treated very differently than the men. They were provided minimal facilities and had separate entrances to lecture halls and dining rooms.

In 2016, it was estimated that 70 percent of all high school valedictorians were girls[8], and that number is trending higher every year. What that means for our girls is that if you excel, create the perfect CV for the college admissions team, take all the AP courses you can, volunteer in your community, and ace your SATs and ACTs, you can still lose your top college spot because universities strive to maintain a 60/40 gender balance.

I fear that top-tier universities that 50 years ago resisted admitting women now are turning away highly qualified female applicants because of their gender because too many young women are outperforming their male peers.

But even if women completed their business degrees, the laws often prevented them from advancing in the business world, accessing capital, and keeping their own wages.

Business loans were not available to women until 1988, with the passage of the Women's Business Ownership Act. In 1974, the Equal Credit Opportunity Act passed. Before that, women needed a man to cosign for any lines of credit. But it wasn't until 1988 that it was illegal to require a male relative to cosign a business loan.

Before researching this book, I was unfamiliar with "coverture," a term that considers a married household to be a single legal and financial entity. This was eventually understood to mean the woman was also the property of her husband. Women were not legally allowed to own property or keep wages they had independently earned. In 1839, Mississippi passed a law that let women have property in their own names and in 1848, New York passed a similar law and added a provision for women to keep separately their own

---

[8]Fugler.

wages. By 1865, more than half of the United States had laws in place allowing women to independently manage and earn their own money, property, and inheritances.

Such an intruder on the rights of men

—*Countess of Winchilsea Anne Finch*, "The Introduction"

Until 1978, pregnancy was a valid reason a woman could be fired from her job in the United States. That year, Congress amended the Civil Rights Act to include sex discrimination in employment, stating that women affected by pregnancy, birth, or related medical conditions be treated the same as all other employees. It took until 1993 for the Family Medical Leave Act (FMLA) to become law, requiring employers to guarantee parents employment after 12 weeks of unpaid leave following the birth or adoption of a child, or to tend to any other serious medical condition of a family member.

The FMLA was the first acknowledgment of the equal standing of men and women in the workplace and at home, as well as the demands on many single-parent households. The United States is still one of the few developed nations that does not provide paid leave under the law, and unpaid leave is not affordable for many lower income workers.

Minimum wage laws in the United States also disproportionately affect women. Women hold two-thirds of minimum wage jobs while also managing 77 percent of single-parent households and often hold several simultaneous minimum wage jobs. Working full time (35+ hours) at minimum wage, currently $7.25 per hour before taxes, brings home less than $15,000 per year. Minimum wage jobs can no longer be seen as transitional, temporary, or training for higher wage jobs. In 2011, less than 12 percent of minimum wage jobs were held by teenagers. The average age for a minimum wage worker is 35. Most work full time. Most are parents. As of 2013, there are approximately 3.3 million people working at or below the federal minimum wage of $7.25 per hour in the United States.[9]

The National Employment Law Project reports that in 2015, 63 percent of Americans were in favor of increasing the national minimum wage to $15 per hour, and 75 percent were in favor of increasing it to $12.50 (it has been $7.25 per hour since 2009). The $2.13 minimum wage for tipped servers has not increased since 1991, when it was $2.09. The first minimum wage was set in 1938 as part of the New Deal under the Fair Labor Standards Act under President Franklin D. Roosevelt. A full-time, year-round minimum wage job could keep a family of two above the poverty line between the mid-1960s through the mid-1980s. But raises to the federal minimum wage have been blocked or stalled throughout most of the past 40 years, so that is no longer possible.

Equal pay for equal work endures as a challenge for women in the workplace. Congress passed an Equal Pay law in 1963, but it took until 1972 for the law to extend into white collar positions. And it wasn't until 1968 that it became illegal to specify gender within a help wanted ad. During World War II, women filled the industrial production line jobs in lieu of men who were serving abroad. The National War Labor Board, a government agency developed

---

[9]Bureau of Labor Statistics.

to prevent work stoppages due to labor disputes during wartime, encouraged companies to pay women the same rate that was paid to the men who previously held those jobs. But their recommendation had no teeth, so most employers ignored it. And when the veterans returned from war, they resumed their previous jobs and the women were again without jobs.

In recent years, several high-profile companies have publicly announced their intent to fix the gender wage gap, most notably software giant Salesforce, which, in 2015, under CEO Marc Benioff, committed to upleveling the company's pay structure so that women were on par with men. Since that announcement, it's estimated that it has put over $6 million toward fixing the problem (it is an ongoing issue due to acquisitions). It's also worth noting that this initiative was launched by two senior women at Salesforce—they long suspected a gap and brought it to Benioff. His initial skepticism was not enough to stop the evaluation, and it has been a watershed for the organization.

Salesforce also has an internal awareness campaign called Women's Surge, through which the company hopes to hire and promote more women into leadership. On its most basic level, Women's Surge requires that 30 percent of all meeting attendees are women. I'd love to see this practice not only be adopted more widely throughout corporate America, but be expanded to include other diverse populations, particularly as it reflects the population each company seeks to serve.

Seeing the strong marketing and public relations value of the Salesforce pay equity initiative, Facebook, Microsoft, Apple, and Intel each quickly followed with public announcements that they had also reached pay parity. But without a deeper transparency into their hiring, promotions, executive diversity, and retention, it has been challenging to verify.

California (where Salesforce is based, incidentally) in October of 2018, under Governor Jerry Brown, passed the first law requiring that publicly traded companies with executive locations in their state have at least one woman on their board of directors by the end of 2019; two if they have five directors; and, by the end of 2021, three if they have seven directors. This will create 692 board seats for women in California by 2021, according to a Bloomberg study,[10] and, if that law were to be adopted by every state, there would be a minimum of 3,732 board seats held by women. Of the 445 publicly traded companies, about 25 percent don't have a woman on the board. Opposition to the law has been strong, and it will be interesting to track both adoption and success, as well as how many other states pass similar legislation.

Fewer than 25 percent of working women have pensions, and while more women tend to participate in employer sponsored 401(k) plans, their savings tend to be smaller and accrue more slowly. If a woman contributes 5 percent of her income to a 401(k) plan, into which her employer matches 5 percent each year, but her earnings are lower, those compounded earnings will take longer to grow. Also, if she takes time out from her career to support her family, that pause will not only lower her lifetime contributions and employer match, but the rate at which she will gain interest will be affected over the life of the account.

This is also why the recent legislation in seven states that prevents employers from asking about previous salary history is so critical for women. If women are hired at lower pay rates, which are then carried forward with each subsequent employer, their ability to accumulate wealth and savings is continuously limited. During the past decade, the average pay raise has been between 2 to 5 percent. For example, a woman hired at $50,000 gets a 2.5 percent raise each year and then gets hired by another employer. That new employer could have paid her $75,000, but because of her prior salary history,

---

[10]Green.

brings her in at just over $55,000. That has a significant impact on her lifetime earnings and her compounded interest.

As one of his first actions as president, Barack Obama in January of 2009 signed into law the Lilly Ledbetter Fair Pay Act (LLFPA), which states that the 180-day statute of limitations for filing an equal-pay lawsuit regarding pay discrimination resets with each new paycheck affected by that discriminatory action. In layman's terms, Lilly Ledbetter was denied a fair pay complaint before the Supreme Court because she filed outside of the previous 180-day restriction, even though she hadn't learned of the discriminatory practices at Goodyear, her employer, until she was close to retirement. The LLFPA removed the 180-day restriction, recognizing that many pay practices are confidential and the 180-day restriction was unreasonable and would disproportionately affect women.

Lilly Ledbetter has never received restitution from Goodyear.

A Timeline of Parity for Women in the Workplace

I was probably in my late twenties when it occurred to me that every law, every entitlement in the United States was created by and for and given—exclusively—to white men. Through legislation, protests, tenacity, hard work, and cleverness, the rest of us have made slow and steady progress.

In researching this book, I wanted to know exactly how long it took for women—or a woman, in many instances—to achieve parity with men in various fields. In doing so, I wasn't able to always draw a 1:1 parallel—nor did I have access to data regarding what these women were paid once they reached a level equal to men. Regardless, I hope this information provides a sense of how long it has taken, and will take, for women to get on equal footing with men.

Publishing

1855: Anne McDowell was the first American woman to publish a newspaper completely run by women; it was circulated weekly and titled *Women's Advocate.*

1690: *Publick Occurrences, Both Forreign and Domestick,* the first newspaper published in America, was printed in Boston by Richard Pierce and edited by Benjamin Harris.

Years between male and female achievement: 165

Law

1869: Arabella Mansfield was the first female lawyer in America; she was admitted to the Iowa bar in 1869.

1776: Of the 56 white male signers of the Declaration of Independence, 25 were lawyers. Of the 55 white male framers of the Constitution, 32 were lawyers.

Years between male and female achievement: 93

Presidential Campaigns

1872: Victoria Woodhull was the first woman to run for President of the United States.

1972: Shirley Chisholm was the first black woman to run for president, and the first woman to run for president in the Democratic party (she did not receive the party's nomination).

2016: Hillary Clinton was the first woman to be nominated by and run for president under a major party.

1789: George Washington was elected president (uncontested).

Years between male and female achievement: 227

US Cabinet Appointments

1933: Frances Perkins was the first woman to serve as a cabinet member and, as such, the first woman to serve as Secretary of Labor.

1789: The first Cabinet—four members—was all men.

1913: The first male Secretary of Labor was appointed.

Years between male and female achievement: 144

Corporate Governance

1934: Lettie Pate Whitehead was the first woman to serve as a director of a major corporation (the Coca-Cola Company).

1813: Boston Manufacturing Co., the first US factory, was founded. Although banks had been founded before this, they were not considered corporations until shortly after the American Revolution.

Years between male and female achievement: 121

Wall Street

1964: Isabel Benham was the first female partner in R.W. Pressprich & Co.'s 55-year history, which also made her the first female partner at any Wall Street bond house.

1842: Jay Cooke was the first investment banker in the United States.

Years between male and female achievement: 122

New York Stock Exchange

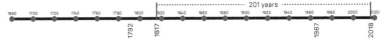

2018: Stacey Cunningham was named the 67th President of the NYSE and the first woman to hold the position.

1967: Muriel Siebert was the first female member.

1817: Anthony Stockholm became the first President of the NYSE.

1792: NYSE was founded by 24 brokers, originally known as The Buttonwood Agreement.

Years between male and female achievement: 201

Fortune 500 CEOs

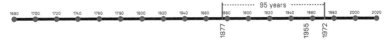

1972: Katharine Graham was the first female Fortune 500 CEO, as CEO of the Washington Post Company.

1955: Fortune 500 list is first published.

1877: *Washington Post*, led by men, is first published.

Years between male and female achievement: 95

US Governor

1974: Ella T. Grasso was elected governor of Connecticut, the first woman to be elected as a governor who was not the wife or widow of a governor.

1924: Nellie Tayloe Ross sworn in as governor of Wyoming in a special election after her husband died in office.

1909: In accordance with Oregon state law, Carolyn Shelton, a personal secretary to two-term Governor Chamberlain, assumes governorship of Oregon for the 49 hours between Chamberlain leaving for DC to be sworn in as a senator and his Secretary of State being sworn in as his replacement for governor.

1769: Jonathan Trumbull serves as governor of the colony of Connecticut.

Years between male and female achievement: 205

Acceptance into Military Academies

1976: Women admitted to service academies under President Gerald Ford. 119 women became the first women cadets at West Point when they joined the Class of 1980. 62 would graduate.

1995: First female valedictorian at West Point was Rebecca E. Marier.

2017: Cadet Simone Askew assumed the post of First Captain at West Point, the highest position in the cadets' chain of command. She is the first African American female to hold the position.

1802: West Point was established.

Years between male and female achievement: 174

Nobel Prize—Individual Award

1977: Barbara McClintock was the first woman to win an unshared Nobel Prize in Physiology or Medicine. She was the first American woman to do so.

1901: First Nobel Prizes were awarded.

Years between male and female achievement: 76

Ivy League President

1994: Judith Rodin was the first permanent female president of an Ivy League University—specifically, the University of Pennsylvania (UPenn).

1740: University of Pennsylvania was founded.

1701: Reverend Abraham Pierson was the first Yale president.

Years between male and female achievement: 293

Fortune 50 CEO

1999: Carly Fiorina was the first woman to lead a Fortune 50 company (Hewlett-Packard).

1988: HP, led by a man, first appears on the Fortune 50.

1955: Fortune 500 list is first published. All companies were led by male CEOs.

Years between male and female achievement: 44

Automotive

2013: General Motors named Mary Barra as its first female CEO and the first female CEO of a major automaker.

1886: Durant-Dort Carriage Company first major multibrand car company founded by William Durant.

Years between male and female achievement: 127

Naval Admiral

2014: Michelle J. Howard began her assignment as the US Navy's first female and first female African American four-star admiral on July 1.

1866: David Farragut was promoted to admiral from vice admiral.

Years between male and female achievement: 148

Laura Okmin

"Women supporting women in this business is magic."

Every NFL Sunday, Laura Okmin is on the field with the players and coaches, ready to interview whoever makes the great play or the wild fumble that day. As a woman over 40 in a sport that prefers women who smile, cheer, and show their midriffs, she has earned her place. And now she's committed to making sure other women get there too.

In 2015, she started losing assignments to a younger female reporter. Rather than being bitter, she sought a way to help the fans see the value in both younger women rising in the field and women with years of experience, who brought deep knowledge and strong relationships to the sideline experience. "It's not fair to compare me to a woman 15 years younger than me and it's also not fair for her to be compared to someone who has two decades of experience on her. It's unfair to both women. You find the value in both women. There's room for both ... and so much value in both."

When she got her first on camera assignment at an Alabama football game in the early '90s, the coaches hardly took Okmin seriously. Her Chicago childhood, spent in a city that fielded at least one professional team—sometimes two—in every major sport, and with a mother who encouraged her to learn all she could about sports, gave her confidence and credibility on the field. But her gender forced her to prove herself and her knowledge, and to earn respect.

And other women from whom she could draw guidance were scarce.

When they think your softness is your weakness

—*Nikita Gill*, "Fire"

B eing a woman in sports broadcasting was hardly anything new, but their scarcity and the lack of community among them made it impossible for them to learn from and encourage each other. Mentors were empathic men who had enough power within their organizations to give women positions with decision-making authority and power.

In 2016, Roger Goodell, the NFL Commissioner, hosted the first-ever Women's Summit for two days before Super Bowl 50. Prior to this, and only since 2009, has the League done anything targeted specifically to its female fans, specifically when the field and players turn pink to raise awareness for breast cancer during October. (That campaign, which has raised a paltry $15 million through sales of pink NFL merchandise, has since been expanded to all detectable cancers and left to each team's discretion to select.)

The three Women's Summits that have been held so far have gotten scathing reviews for being more marketing than substance, with lots of pink in the conference rooms and men on stage telling women in the audience how much they respect women. Doing something is generally better than doing nothing, but this seems so far like it's been a patronizing, pandering attempt to check a box that says WOMEN, use the summit for a nice public relations lift, and move on.

Women often hear that they can't really know the game as they haven't played it at a competitive level. In October of 2017, Cam Newton of the Carolina Panthers chided *Charlotte Observer* beat reporter Jourdan Rodrigue, who is a woman, when he said, "It's funny to hear a female talk about routes. It's funny."

Rodrigue privately challenged Newton that he didn't know what she saw, or what she knew. He admitted, when she asked, that he didn't even know her name or that she had covered the team every day for over a year for the local Charlotte paper. Newton never apologized to Rodrigue.

---

the gladdest things in the toyroom
—*May Swenson*, "Women"

Title IX, the 1972 law that prohibits sex discrimination in any school that receives federal funding, among other rights, gave women equal access to school-sponsored athletics:

"No person in the United States shall, on the basis of sex, be excluded from participation in, be denied the benefits of, or be subjected to discrimination under any education program or activity receiving federal financial assistance."[11]

Prior to Title IX, it was mostly men who were the ones given collegiate scholarships. Most athletic budgets gave only 1 percent to female sports. Male high school athletes outnumbered females 12.5 to 1. According to the Women's Sports Foundation, the dramatic increase in women's athletic participation since Title IX was passed in 1972 (by 560 percent at the college level and 990 percent in high schools) proves that lack of opportunity kept females out of competitive athletic participation.[12]

Six times as many high school girls were participating in competitive high school sports in 1978 than had done so in 1970. The budget for women's sports at North Carolina State had multiplied by 15 in just four years. The University of Michigan had not had a single formal competitive sport for women in 1973; five years later, it had 10 varsity teams for them.

In 1974, Connie Carberg got a job as a secretary in the scouting office of the New York Jets. Like Laura Okmin, she grew up loving the sport and, specifically, the Jets. Her father and uncles were the team doctors, which only fed her interest and passion. At Ohio State University, Carberg was mentored by legendary football coach Woody Hayes, whom she credits with teaching her how to recognize great players.

When she started with the Jets, she knew more about scouting than she did about secretarial work. It didn't take long for the Jets front office to notice Carberg's ability to see talent in players. At 24,

---

[11]United States Department of Justice.
[12]Women's Sports Foundation.

she became the NFL's first female scout in 1975, while also staying in her position as team secretary.

"I didn't go into sports with an intention of making a splash or creating a headline. If anything, I wanted to be more invisible so I didn't create a distraction for my beloved team." At that time, all of her mentors were men. And Carberg will proudly tell you she'd not have gotten anywhere without them. She came to be known affectionately around the league as "the Girl Scout."

In her biggest contribution to the Jets franchise, she found Mark Gastineau in sleepy East Central Oklahoma, and the Jets drafted him on her recommendation in 1979. Gastineau went on to be a five-time Pro Bowler, led the league in sacks twice, and was named Defensive Player of the Year in 1982. Meanwhile, Carberg's scouting career was halted in 1978 when new owner Leon Hess took over and stated that he didn't want a woman traveling with the team.

And tries to forget it has dreamed of the stars
—*Georgia Douglas Johnson*, "The Heart of a Woman"

One of Laura Okmin's closest friends was her colleague Stuart Scott, the beloved ESPN SportsCenter anchor. They worked together during their early careers and became close friends as both of their careers took flight along parallel trajectories. Scott was not the network's first African American anchor, but his style and warmth changed forever the way we all talk about sports. At first, his style was controversial, but it worked because, for the first time, fans heard an anchor talk about sports like a fan. It also brought criticism, racism, hate mail, and threats. But Scott was authentically himself, and his fans and the network stuck with him. He talked to viewers from the anchor desk the way they talked with each other during games. And no one had done that in quite that way before him.

Being the first, or one of the few, is risky and makes you a target. Okmin and Scott found in each other a strong friendship that endured over the years, and a trusted ally upon which they could lean and draw much needed support. Scott was the first national sportscaster who was relatable to African Americans (70 percent of NFL players and 75 percent of NBA players are black), and Okmin likes to think her method of reporting also makes the game more approachable to the 45 percent of fans who are women. That number increases every year, and she knows having more women representing every role on and off the field is important— not only to female fans but also to the men who participate in and watch faithfully every week.

The NFL definitely has issues with women, some of which are being addressed, and some are well beyond the purview of the organization.

For years, the rumored replacement of Roger Goodell was Condoleeza Rice, former National Security Advisor and Secretary of State in George W. Bush's administration. Rice herself in 2002 stated that NFL Commissioner would be her dream job. Appointing a woman to the top post would certainly invite some necessary systemic changes to the organization.

In 2016, Goodell announced an extension of the Rooney Rule, which requires all NFL teams to interview at least one minority candidate for any open coaching position and that women were to be interviewed for open executive positions in the League office. It's a start, and will lead the way for more women in leadership across the League.

The NFL reported in 2016 that there were 31 women at the vice president level and above, and in 2018 they promoted Maryann Turcke to Chief Operating Officer. Thirty percent of front office employees are women, and 26.5 percent of all vice presidents at the League office are women.[13]

Sarah Thomas became the first woman to be hired as a full-time game official in 2015. And in 2017, Beth Mowins called the play-by-play on Monday Night Football's opening weekend alongside Rex Ryan, the former coach and broadcasting novice that night. It was the first time a woman called a nationally televised game. Minutes before kickoff, the voiceover on SportsCenter announced: "This particular doubleheader is especially meaningful. It also signals to female sports journalists and budding female broadcasters that a career in sports is a legitimate possibility. Because this Monday, regardless of gender, the most qualified person has been given the job." It's worth noting that Rex Ryan completely bombed that night, but Twitter seemed more concerned with discussing how Mowins's voice was "annoying" them.

In 2018, Amazon Video announced that their Thursday night live broadcast—the first live sports to be hosted on a streaming service—would be anchored by two women, Hannah Storm and Andrea Kremer. Unfortunately, their historic broadcast was ruined by technical issues when fans couldn't find the game on Amazon. Both Storm and Kremer are coming back for the 2019 season.

But, as any of the First Club members will attest, influence and power are not immediately granted based only on title and position. When Condoleeza Rice was provost at Stanford University and

---

[13]Freeman.

oversaw the budget for the athletic department, she participated in the hiring process for new coaches. Like Connie Carberg, she would frequently surprise candidates with the depth of her understanding of the game.

The space for women in the NFL is still very small, but I see it widening. From the voiceless cheerleaders of my childhood in the 1970s to the present day, when the Buffalo Bills hired their first female coach, and four women are 100 percent of NFL team owners, we are achieving positions of greater control and influence over a sport for which we hold 45 percent of viewership.

who in the hell set things up like this

—*June Jordan*, "Poem About My Rights"

TV work is incredibly competitive, and women's looks are constantly scrutinized. Executives at Fox News are known to comment more on their female anchors' hair, makeup, and wardrobe than their reporting.

To succeed on camera past 40 is becoming less remarkable for women, but it's still a significant accomplishment. When Okmin saw her airtime being given to a younger, less experienced female reporter, she chose to turn it into another opportunity. Realizing that her experience could benefit younger women and make them better at their jobs, she did something incredible.

In 2012, Okmin founded GALvanize, a two-day intensive bootcamp for up and coming women sports professionals. She wanted women to have the necessary confidence and knowledge to be credible on air. She wanted to build a community of women who would support each other, share knowledge and opportunities with each other, and build each other up in an industry that tells them that they don't know anything, that they aren't hot enough, that they don't belong.

For younger women building their careers in sports reporting, Okmin became the mentor that she didn't have. She realized how little preparation and training these women had and how that was setting them up for eventual failure. She knew the impact this would have on other women in the industry. As she says, "Men ask stupid questions, but we're stupid."

Each session pairs the women with a professional team, putting them nose to nose with players and coaches. They study games, reports, and players, and prepare questions for the following day's interviews. They meet women across all of the business and team functions—coaches, analysts, finance, operations, promotions. The women discuss attire and image, but focus more heavily on confidence—she wants every woman to leave her program more confident than she arrived. Her goal is to teach lasting skills so the women can grow into respected, trusted reporters, who, as Okmin likes to say, have relationships, not sources, a critical difference in how to cultivate a professional network.

The program has had an immensely positive impact on the careers of many of its graduates, and Okmin has seen changes in the women over the two-day program. If you follow her and GALvanize on social media, she shares the wonderful ways the women not only reflect on their learnings with GALvanize but the bonds they've built with each other. Improved poise both on and off camera, confidence in their knowledge of the game, confidence approaching the players after both good and bad plays, and the sisterhood they build among the class are things they will carry into any career they choose. When the women display true authenticity, Okmin is satisfied that her program will have lasting impact on the women, the fans, and the league.

Arlan Hamilton

"How much of a fist in the air would it be to just be obnoxiously wealthy as a gay black woman? And to be able to help other people do the same?"

In 2015, Arlan Hamilton was determined to launch a venture capital fund to invest in women, people of color, LGBT, and other underserved founders. Problem was, no one was calling her back. She was an unknown in Silicon Valley and her pitch wasn't landing. But she knew there was money to be made investing in the stuff the white heterosexual males overlooked. She saw people with great ideas not getting meetings because they didn't fit the profile. Neither did she—as a black, gay woman without a college degree, a permanent address, and with very little money.

It's now 2019, and she's running her own venture capital fund—Backstage Capital. And she recently announced that she is hoping to increase her investment in black female founders to $1 million each, a total investment of $36 million. She's calling it the It's About Damn Time Fund.

Hamilton has been on the cover of *Fast Company* magazine, the first black woman on their cover who was not an entertainer or athlete. When I first started following her, I predicted that she'd soon be a Harvard Business School case study. Even the Backstage Capital homepage looks nothing like those of other VC firms.

Until very recently, venture capital firms have almost exclusively been full of white men investing in other white men.

In a study of 7,000 companies conducted jointly by research teams at Wellesley College and Babson College, female CEOs raised just 3 percent of venture capital funding—$1.5 billion of a total $50.8 billion between 2011 and 2013.[14] In their 2019 annual Women in Leadership study, Silicon Valley Bank reported that half of startups have no women on their leadership teams[15] while 28 percent have at least one woman on their founding team.

Firms with women on their executive teams raised lower funding than those with all men, and those with all men were four times more likely to get any VC funding at all.[16] And women of color? They received only about 0.2 percent of all available funding.

If women aren't on the investment teams, fewer women-owned businesses will even be considered. In 2016, it was estimated that only 7 percent of the investing partners at the top 100 firms were women. In 2017, eight of those firms added a female partner for the first time. Women work in venture capital, just not in positions of power and influence. They number 45 percent of the VC workforce, but only about 11 percent are investment partners.

Perhaps the best known and respected woman in the high stakes high-profile VC world is Mary Meeker who recently left Kleiner Perkins (where she had been since 2010) to start her own firm. She's known as much for her eagerly anticipated annual Internet Trends Report as her investment track record, although both are impressive. Meeker was one of the first Wall Street analysts to

---

[14]Brush, Greene, Balachandra, and Davis, "Gender gap."
[15]Silicon Valley.
[16]Babson College.

see the future in desktop computing and Internet commerce back in the '90s.

According to *Fortune Magazine*, 5,839 male-founded companies got VC funding in 2016, or 16 times more funding than female-founded companies.[17] And the data show that while more female founders are being funded, deal sizes are lower, so the actual capital going to women is shrinking. Because so many investment decisions are made from a homogenous team of partners, they are limited in evaluating the viability of an idea beyond their own experience.

Arlan Hamilton's first investor was Susan Kimberlin, former PayPal and Salesforce executive and now an angel investor who believes strongly in diversity as a corporate asset. Hamilton met Kimberlin at a 500 Startups cohort where of the 30 startups, 15 were women and the women were offered a 50 percent discount on tuition. It was through this cohort that Kimberlin realized she wanted to go bullish on angel investing. And so, when Hamilton called looking for an investment, Kimberlin called back.

Kimberlin had worked for Salesforce on a team of 70, only three of whom were women. As strong as Salesforce is in being mindful of diversity and inclusion, she experienced isolation the higher she rose into leadership. She felt her career had stalled, her input wasn't welcome, and the feedback she got from her peers was generic and not helping her grow. When she left Salesforce, she knew she wanted to work on increasing inclusion in technology.

Her first experience with angel investing was with Arlan Hamilton. She believed strongly in the social impact of Hamilton's work and saw the massive economic opportunity other investors were overlooking. Hamilton's mission fit squarely with Kimberlin's investment goals. Kimberlin felt like she was investing in Hamilton, not just the vision. She became her first investor with a

---

[17]Zarya.

$25,000 check. Kimberlin's investment portfolio is now 30 percent in underrepresented founders, or businesses that seek to solve diversity and inclusion.

I know I have not ground you down enough
—*Elizabeth Barrett Browning*, Aurora Leigh

To get to the reasons for funding disparity, the Diana Project out of Babson College has studied women founders and those who invest in women. They first conducted the study in 1999 and reported some significant positive changes between then and when they ran it again in 2014 using the same methodology.

Among the findings, women founders tended to receive the most funding when they were in the health and medical sectors, and the least in telecommunications, semiconductors, and IT services. Women partners at VC firms declined as a percentage from 10 percent in 1999 to 6 percent in 2014. When women are partners, their firms are three times more likely to invest in a woman CEO.[18]

According to the Small Business Administration, women are majority owners in 36 percent of all small businesses, and about one in 10 women in the United States are entrepreneurs. But the Diana Project found that only 2.7 percent (183 of 6,517) of companies that received venture capital funding had a woman CEO.

---

[18]Brush.

The increasing number of women partners in VC firms is definitely having an impact, as is the number of women starting their own funds like Hamilton. But she shared with me an astute prediction: soon, companies will build out diverse management teams not only because it's the right thing to do, but because it will make them more attractive to investors looking for more diverse portfolios. She believes that in the next two years, there will be a significant exit—when an investor sells their shares at a substantial profit—for a person of color in the tech sector, which will immediately get the attention of the ecosystem. Tons of investors will look to copy that investment opportunity. And Hamilton likes to tell people, "Get your buckets out and catch the rain."

Hamilton started learning about tech investing in 2013, when she was working as a tour manager. She dove into the space, reading, watching talks, and eventually interviewing her new heroes to learn as much as she could from the people at the top of their game. She wrote about what she learned in a Medium post titled "Dear White Venture Capitalists."[19]

Among the more memorable lines from her post:

"Do the same thing you do with white and Asian founders and invest in them because you want to make money. Do not think of this as a social mission."

"Because of the blind spot investors have for this group of people right now, there's an enormous opportunity to invest at undervalued prices. It won't always be this way."

It went viral, and the VC firms started calling her. But not with anything substantial. They wanted to tap her knowledge and her

---

[19]Hamilton.

networks. She knew she was better on her own. So, with less than $20,000 in funding for 1 percent ownership, she started investing a little at a time in firms she had discovered. Her goal was to invest in 100 companies by 2020, and she's well on her way. By August of 2017, she had invested in her 50th company, only two years after officially launching. And by May of 2019, Backstage Capital had invested $5 million in 100 startups.

Backstage Capital has not changed its core mission. As of this writing, 72 percent of their investments are companies run by people of color, 62 percent are companies founded by women, and 44 percent are founded by women of color. Companies with LGBTQ founders round it out at 12 percent of the total. As a gay black woman, Hamilton wants to see the number of investments in LGBTQ founders get to 20 percent by 2020. Fewer than 2 percent are run by heterosexual white men. Looking at the Backstage Capital portfolio page is a visual confirmation that diversity is a solid investment strategy, and one that is poised to erupt.

Susan Kimberlin, Hamilton's first $25,000 investor, became a General Partner with Backstage Capital. She does a lot of work for Backstage Capital now to get them connected and in front of the right audiences. The work that Hamilton and Backstage Capital are doing is already changing the investment conversation across the industry, and far outside of tech.

Must your light like mine be hidden
—*Christina Rossetti*, "Goblin Market"

Women have always struggled to be taken seriously in finance, on both the business and personal sides. Muriel Siebert, a Jewish woman, was the first woman to buy a seat on NYSE in 1967, and remained the only woman (among 1,375 men) for the next decade. She faced opposition and hostility from the others on the trading floor. In 1977, she became the first woman Superintendent of Banking for the State of New York, overseeing about $500 billion. Not one bank failed during her term, a time when many banks around the country were failing and interest rates were rising. Siebert succeeded in the municipal bond business because many cities, states, and counties insisted that a woman-owned firm be among the syndicate of firms issuing their bonds.

She once had to enter the famous Union League Club through the kitchen for a lunch meeting while her male peers walked through the front door.[20] She was so irritated, her male peers tried to bring her into the elevator with them as they left. The Union League Club wouldn't allow it, so the men walked out the back stairs with her.[21] She fought for women to be allowed memberships to these exclusive clubs, believing that many important business deals and conversations occurred there. She successfully lobbied the NYSE to install a women's restroom next to the luncheon club, rather than on another floor. She was tireless in taking on injustices.

She donated millions to seed women in business and finance. Half of her firm's profits were also shared with charities through Siebert Entrepreneurial Philanthropic Plan. Long before Warren Buffett, Chan Zuckerberg, and the Bill and Melinda Gates Foundation, she saw the power of giving back into her community to help others in material, measurable ways. Through this fund, she funded

---

[20]Ickeringill.
[21]Nemy.

various women-oriented charities chosen by the bond beneficiaries. She created a program to improve financial literacy in high school age children, which started in New York City but was then adopted in schools across the United States.

This prescient quote from Siebert should be etched into the hallways of every financial institution across the globe:

> "Men at the top of industry and government should be more willing to risk sharing leadership with women and minority members who are not merely clones of their white male buddies. In these fast-changing times we need the different viewpoints and experiences, we need the enlarged talent bank. The real risk lies in continuing to do things the way they've always been done."[22]

Siebert Hall at the New York Stock Exchange was dedicated in 2016 in honor of her. This was the first time a room at the New York Stock Exchange was named after an individual. And in May of 2018, Stacey Cunningham was named the 67th President of the NYSE, the first woman to hold that position.

Do not think I underestimate your great concern.
—*Sylvia Plath*, "Lady Lazarus"

---

[22]Your Dictionary, "Muriel Siebert Facts."

In 2015, the National Venture Capital Association acknowledged the lack of diversity among its members, so it established a task force "to develop a clear and measurable path to increase opportunities for women and men of diverse backgrounds to thrive in venture capital and entrepreneurship."[23] Of 11 seats on the task force, seven were white men. None were people of color.

The first venture capital firms grew out of successful early technology companies' founders seeding the ancillary companies started by former employees. The original eight men who founded Fairchild Semiconductor went on to support companies that became Intel and AMD. Names that endure today are Eugene Kleiner, who started Kleiner Perkins in 1972, and Don Valentine who launched Sequoia Capital. Recent research by Endeavor Insight traces 92 publicly traded companies back to the Fairchild team, valued at about $2.1 trillion.[24]

All eight of the Fairchild Semiconductor founders were white men. And within their initial investors were a group known as Rockefeller Brothers, even though their sister Abigail—the oldest of the siblings and the only girl—was an investor. (She focused more on philanthropy than investing, but her obituary notes that she established a fund at the Massachusetts Institute of Technology for a woman professor in a field in which women were underrepresented, the Abby Rockefeller Mauze Professor of the Social Studies of Science and Technology.)

The homogeneous culture of venture capital is deeply rooted and largely formed by a mirrortocracy—when an organization recruits, mentors, promotes, and supports those who look like its leaders. We are naturally drawn to those with whom we feel we have the most in common. It is easier to connect and relate to people who went to your school, who grew up under similar circumstances, in

[23]Veghte.
[24]Morris and Penido.

whom you see your younger self reflected. Conversations are easier, connections are smooth, references are shared.

The PayPal Mafia[25] is the 20 or so men who built and funded PayPal and went on to other highly successful technology companies, oftentimes with each other. They have directly touched about 400 companies since 2002, and their investment funds have seeded thousands of others. Since many of these companies are privately held, it's impossible to quantify their financial impact, but the impact on the innovation and success throughout the sector, and in particular in Silicon Valley, is massive. There are no women among them, and they have invested in very few companies founded by women. This leaves one homogenous group to design and program the future world in which we will all live—and accumulate the profits while doing so.

Another element that works against many founders from lower socioeconomic backgrounds is their financial literacy. Financial literacy can be defined as having attained mastery in the following areas: savings, budgeting, investing, credit management, and understanding retirement strategies and mortgaging. Mastery is essential to anyone wanting to accumulate wealth. And the earlier children are exposed to the language and concepts around personal finance, the more adept they will be as adults navigating successfully their own credit, debt, and investment decisions.

Children's ability to understand theoretical financial concepts is limited, much as their understanding of today versus next year is limited. When presented with 100 pennies or 10 dimes, smaller children will choose the pennies based solely on volume, not value. The first opportunity for a child to understand money is usually when they want something and are told they have to earn it.

Angel Rich wants to make the language of finance available to everyone, for free. In July 2016, she launched CreditStacker, a

---

[25]Fleximize.

game geared toward kids that interactively shows them how to build credit, pay down debt, and accumulate wealth. Players move through various life stages and a soundtrack explains the hows and whys of building good credit. Points are accumulated for paying off debt, making good financial decisions, and answering correctly a series of questions related to personal credit.

Over 250,000 people downloaded the app within two weeks of its launch, and it was named the Best Learning Game by the Department of Education in December 2016.

Rich's mother gave her business books when she was young. Her parents were in life insurance and raised her with a mind for finance. After growing up in Washington, DC, Rich went on to Hampton University, a historically black college in Hampton, Virginia, and home to Emancipation Oak, where the first southern reading of the Emancipation Proclamation took place. After graduating from Hampton with honors, she started working as an analyst at Prudential.

While working for Prudential, Rich went to Kenya on a mission trip, where she met a young local boy in a Wharton T-shirt. Knowing the slim chance that boy had of ever attending Wharton, she quit Prudential and turned her focus to financial literacy for kids.

She launched the Wealth Factory in 2013 to develop tools for financial literacy through online gaming, adaptive testing, and other means.

I am treacherous with old magic
—*Audre Lorde*, "A Woman Speaks"

Accerding to the Federal Deposit Insurance Corporation (FDIC), 20 percent of US households (24.5 million) were "underbanked" in 2015, relying primarily on cash or checks over credit cards or loans, while 7 percent (9 million) were unbanked. These are mostly low-income households, that either don't earn enough money to maintain a minimum balance or want to avoid fees assessed by banks. This leads to higher incidences of theft, fraud, and abuse, riskier decisions, and lower overall savings for almost 30 percent of the US population. The majority of these households are black, Hispanic, disabled, lower educated, and younger.[26]

PricewaterhouseCoopers (PwC), the global services firm, in 2012 pledged $100 million in volunteer hours and $90 million in cash toward helping educators get more comfortable teaching kids about money and research to determine what methods lead to deeper understanding and implementation as adults. Their research shows that 46 percent of teens do not know how to create a personal budget and close to 50 percent don't know how to correctly use a credit card. Sesame Street Workshop, in partnership with the MetLife Foundation, has launched an international program called Dream Save Do in nine countries to increase financial literacy in families through multimedia educational content.

The financial services industry is known to lack diversity. There's a significantly small portion of minority advisers (6 percent are black, 7.7 percent are Asian, and 7.1 percent are Hispanic), and not many more are women—31.6 percent of all personal financial advisers in 2016 were women, according to the Bureau of Labor Statistics. At the same time, women's wallets and net worth are growing—in 2015, women passed the halfway mark for controlled personal wealth in the United States, according to the Bank of

---

[26]Burhouse et al.

Montreal's Wealth Institute. And by 2020, they're expected to hold $22 trillion.[27]

This presents a multifaceted problem for those of us looking to trust our investments with an advisor: How well does this person know my goals and my current situation? How well can they help me plan for a future they can't see or understand? How seriously do they take me, my questions, and my concerns? For people of color, finding an advisor is even more challenging.

Maggie Lena Walker was born two months after the end of the Civil War. Through her affiliation with the Order of St. Luke, an organization dedicated to the health and advancement of African Americans, she became an activist and advocate, helping the Order of St. Luke grow throughout the United States and provide services to thousands of African Americans. Under the Order of St. Luke, she founded Penny Savings Bank to offer banking services, loans, and mortgages to African Americans, many of whom were turned down by other banks. In doing so, she became the first female bank president. The Penny Savings Bank helped hundreds of families buy their homes and start small businesses.

The intersection of financial security and personal health is being studied with more focus in recent years. Low-income earners suffer higher rates of depression and anxiety, and those who experience income anxiety as children have difficulty adjusting into adulthood. Bankruptcy from health-related crises are on the rise, with even one health setback impacting options for housing and food. Access to affordable health insurance reduces financial anxiety considerably, as seen in studies covering the 10 years since Massachusetts expanded its coverage.[28]

---

[27]Malito.
[28]Mazumder and Miller.

I am the tree that trembles and trembles.

—*Muriel Rukeyser*, "The Speed of Darkness"

Much has been written, studied, and discussed about the lack of diversity in the technology industry. In August of 2017, the Google Manifesto, one man's distasteful reflection on why women don't achieve the same success in technology companies as men, was released. Combined with the rampant sexual harassment cases at companies like Uber and 500 Startups, Americans have been forced to confront misogyny and sexism as deeply rooted values in our culture. Since then, thousands of Google employees staged a walkout in late 2018 to protest Google paying millions to male executives accused of sexual misconduct, the most notable of whom was Andy Rubin. He was paid $90 million even though the harassment claims against him were deemed credible.

The five major technology companies—Google, Facebook, Apple, Amazon, and Twitter—have been asked/forced to release their metrics on women and people of color and the results are abysmal.[29,30] Many of their executive teams and boards are also predominantly white men, like the PayPal Mafia. And self-congratulatory charts about diversity in annual reports are not going to show the true picture of how the demographics of an organization are reflected throughout management ranks.

---

[29]Quick and Tomasevic.
[30]Evans and Rangarajan.

But rather than focus on quickly finding the top woman or minority or whoever to satisfy a demographic split, companies should focus instead on what impact having all white or mostly white men has on their strategy, their offer, and their market. How are they limiting their growth by representing only one world view? No matter how educated, experienced, or intuitive they might be, wouldn't it expand in multipliers if they brought others not like them into the discussion?

Tracy Chadwell, founder of 1843 Capital, believes there needs to be a shift in perception if women founders are to get investment parity from male-led investment firms. She started 1843 Capital—named for the year Ada Lovelace wrote the first computer algorithms—to invest in companies with diverse founders, primarily women. As Chadwell tells me, investing in women holds no more risk than investing in men. In fact, she finds women to be more frugal and deliberate with the dollars invested in them by others, "It's a risk to your reputation, not your return, when you invest in women." Related to Arlan Hamilton's feeling that investing in women and minorities is still seen as philanthropic work, Chadwell wants her successful support of these companies to stand on their own and make investing with women and minority founders the next untapped opportunity.

Every year *Forbes* publishes their Midas List—the top 100 venture capitalists. Mary Meeker, former partner at Kleiner Perkins, widely known for her comprehensive annual "Internet Trends Report", has appeared on the list numerous times, but in the top five only once. The other five women on the 2017 list are ranked at #44 and lower. The good news is there was one additional woman on the 2017 list, a trend that will hopefully continue. Meeker left Kleiner Perkins in late 2018 and launched Bond Capital, and in April of

2019 it became the first female-founded, female-led fund to raise over $1 billion ($1.25 billion, at this writing).[31]

Large companies are also seeing the value of investing in more diverse founders. Intel Capital, the strategic investment arm of Intel Corporation, was founded in 1991 to seed innovation that supports the Intel corporate strategy. To date, they have invested over $12 billion in 1,200 companies all over the world. In 2015, they dedicated $125 million to companies founded by women, veterans, people with disabilities, LGBTQ, and minorities.

Laurence "Lo" Toney, Managing Partner at Plexo Capital, which he spun out from Google Ventures, told me a fascinating story that illustrates perfectly the missed opportunity by homogeneous funders. Diishan Imira founded a hair extension company based in Oakland, California, called Mayvenn. Mayvenn wanted to change the way black women bought hair extensions and provide a way for stylists to sell directly to their clients on commission. But the mostly white funding sources he spoke with didn't understand or didn't believe in the potential for Mayvenn to dramatically change this multibillion-dollar industry. They didn't use the products, they weren't familiar with the market, so they turned him down. In 2013, he got $50,000 from 500 Startups, which ultimately got him close to $2.5 million from investors including Serena Williams.

Toney tells me the best advice for founders is to be singularly passionate about what is the problem you are trying to solve and go deep solving it. The founders he's seen who have been the most successful are those with infectious passion, and are not solely motivated by the money, "Find out what are the rules of engagement with each funding source, and follow those."

---

[31]Clark.

rain will wash away everything if you let it
—*Sarah Kay*, "B"

I t will take time to assess how successful Backstage Capital will be long-term, but one thing is certain. Arlan Hamilton's work and that of many others who are focused on funding women, is forever changing the world of venture capital. What Hamilton is doing, and her approach to doing it, is going to break a lot of models, and we need to give her the space to fail, to learn, to keep improving. And just as importantly, we need to support and foster more Arlan Hamiltons if we want women founders to be funded equitably.

Hamilton knows that the way to bring more women into venture capital is to do what she, Tracy Chadwell, and a growing list of other women in venture capital are doing: build your story from your success. The more minority and women funders and founders demonstrate solid returns, solvent businesses, and smart investment choices, the stronger the story becomes and the identity of the founder is less important than the successes of the strategy.

Kerry Robinson

*"Women belong in positions of leadership in the Catholic
Church not because it's the right thing for women,
but because it is the right thing for the Church."*

I have struggled with how to tell this story, about some really great
work that is happening in and around the Catholic Church, and
how best to present it. I am in no way defending the actions or
the decisions by the Vatican and the Church hierarchy regarding
the rampant sexual abuse of children and women. I am horrified
and disgusted by all of it, and I wrestle daily with my aspiration to
live in the shadow of Jesus Christ and the failings of those we believe
are ordained in His light. I was raised Catholic, by devout Catholic
parents, in a devout Catholic family, in a devout Catholic community, but I have distanced myself from the dogma of the faith. This
seems to be a space in which many Catholics of my generation live—
trying to reconcile our desire to live a life that more closely emulates
that of Jesus with our disdain for the structures and secrecy of the
institution.

So, with that out there, I want to shine a bright light on some
of the work that is happening, diligently and faithfully, on behalf
of all of us, to make the Catholic Church a living, breathing, body
in which we all can find a place of love and acceptance. For those of

you who are not as familiar with the Catholic Church, I hope this chapter inspires you to understand more fully the power of laypeople working from within to transform this powerful organization and the complexity many people, many women, feel and why they remain members of the Church.

The Catholic Church has always been a challenging place for women to feel equally respected alongside men. As someone who was raised in the Catholic tradition, bolstered by 12 years in Catholic schools, Sunday mass, and many sacraments, I'm frustrated by the role of women in the Church compared with the role they play in every other aspect of my life. But this chapter cannot be about my personal experience with the Church. Instead, I wish to share the story of a woman who has a deep commitment to her faith and who has created a place for herself and other women in a highly influential and powerful way.

Kerry Robinson was raised in a family for whom being Catholic was a fundamental principle. Her extended family is bound across generations through a family foundation started by her great grandparents, where they serve as stewards on behalf of the foundation, finding ways to support and strengthen the work of the Church throughout the world.

And today, she is one of the leading voices for women into the Vatican.

Her role with the Leadership Roundtable gives her a literal seat at the table with those who most strongly influence the Pope, his advisors, and, just as importantly, the establishment of accountability standards throughout the Church.

In 2002, when the Catholic Church sex abuse scandal hit the media, Robinson was deeply involved in a $75-million development campaign for Saint Thomas More, the Catholic Chapel and Center at Yale University. Having always been a strong proponent of truth, this revelation about the Church both shattered and inspired her. She knew she had to increase her own participation in the recovery of the Church in order to speak authentically with potential donors about the need to support the Church during this critical time.

One of the first things Robinson and Father Robert Beloin, the late Chaplain at Saint Thomas More, did was organize a conference titled, "Governance, Accountability, and the Future of the Catholic Church" in March of 2003. It was a bold move at a time when the Church was particularly vulnerable. Five hundred attendees listened to 30 speakers from around the world. Participants found the material wrenching, but important, and the organizers kept the focus on transparency, accountability, and improved utilization of the talents from laity. Guests were left feeling hopeful and encouraged.

A few months later, Robinson was attending a meeting for a consortium for Foundations and Donors Interested in Catholic Activities (FADICA), where she listened to a talk by Geoffrey Boisi. Boisi had donated his business talents to Boston College to strengthen their financial position under the college president Father Donald Monan. In the 1970s, the college was deeply in debt and their endowment was thin. This type of partnership between the Jesuit community and lay community was new, having first been implemented by Father Theodore Hesburgh at the University of Notre Dame. Many other Catholic colleges began to follow that model.

Boisi believed strongly in the power of partnering the deep business experience and practices of the lay community with the influence of Catholic leadership in order to create lasting, sustainable change. He was already forming the concept of the Leadership Roundtable when Robinson introduced herself to him at FADICA. Like so many Catholics, the news of the sex abuse scandal was a horrifying surprise to him, and he felt that he was obligated to work to fix it.

Shortly after their chance meeting at FADICA, Robinson organized a meeting with Boisi, Fr. Beloin from St. Thomas More, and Fay Vincent, former Commissioner of Major League Baseball and a lead donor for the Governance conference at St. Thomas More just a few months prior. Soon after this, the Leadership Roundtable, with Robinson as the Executive Director, was born.

What other blessing could be sent?

—Elizabeth Drew Barstow Stoddard, "Nameless Pain"

Contemporaneously with the founding of the Leadership Roundtable, Kerry Robinson served on the advisory board of Voices of Faith, a global platform to amplify the voices of women in the Catholic Church. Founded by Chantal Göetz, Voices of Faith had established trusted relationships in the Vatican, from which Robinson grew advocacy for the Leadership Roundtable and its goal to establish standards, reporting, processes, and best practices throughout the Church.

At first, the Leadership Roundtable was met with skepticism. But their mission was never to expose the Church, nor was it to publicize failings or weaknesses, only to strengthen the Church through a process of discovery and improvement. The Leadership Roundtable team had legacies of service and dedication, which were essential elements for success in launching this modern form of philanthropy, one that drew not from grants or monetary support, but from the deep business expertise and knowledge of laypeople, drawn from all industries, representing Catholics of all genders, all of whom deeply loved the Church and wanted to contribute to its recovery.

The first board meeting of the Leadership Roundtable was an impressive group with intense ideas and powerful personal networks. When devising the talent matrix that drove their recruitment, they found that recruiting talented women at the top of their fields was a challenge, partly because there are so few women in positions of leadership in the private sector, but also because these women are in high demand. Upon evaluating the various opportunities in front of them, many of these women believe the impact they can make in other areas is probably greater than that of the lasting impact their contributions can make to the Church. On the flip side, the perception young Catholic women have of the degree to which the Church values them is not strong.

If the Church is to thrive into the 21st century, elevating women to positions of leadership and decision-making is critically urgent. Robinson sees this changing in the United States, albeit slowly. While not a stated goal of the Leadership Roundtable, increasing the participation of women is a natural outcome of their work, and Robinson is quick to remind those with whom she works that women belong on their teams. It seems the message is seeping through, as a woman, Eleanor Sauers, was named in December of 2018 to lead a parish in Fairfield County, Connecticut—a position of authority traditionally held by a pastor or a priest. The bishop's letter announcing her appointment stated, "It has become apparent to me that many laywomen and men are seeking new ways to serve their parishes and, in collaboration with the clergy, to create vibrant and thriving communities."[32]

---

[32]Caggiano.

When Pope Francis was elected Pope in 2013, his commitment to managerial reform was validation for the mission of Leadership Roundtable, beginning with a thorough audit of the Vatican Bank, led by Robinson's colleague and Leadership Roundtable board member Elizabeth McCaul of Promontory Financial Group. The Pope wants to leave as one of his legacies to the Church the rigor and discipline around the financial and human resource processes and practices at the Vatican. In just a few short years, he has worked toward higher accountability and reporting from the various dicasteries. He established the first Secretariat for the Economy, with oversight for all economic activities for the Vatican, and organizationally, it has equal status to the Secretary of State (that's a big deal). A thorough audit—the first ever (another big deal)—of the Vatican's finances is underway, although it has met with significant resistance from within, even though it has been shown that weaknesses in their systems and processes have left them vulnerable to fraud and even criminal activity, attributable both to lack of knowledge and willful ignorance. Pope Francis wishes to tighten the controls and is leaning on the lay sector for leadership in implementation.

By consolidating the three dicasteries into a single body—the Laity, Family, and Life—he also wrote into the charter that every employee under the Prefect will be a layperson. Robinson and her colleagues provide a talent pipeline of women to this dicastery, and others.

Thou mayst command, but never canst be free.
—*Anna Laetitia Barbauld*, "The Rights of Women"

The role of women in the Catholic faith centers around Mary, the Virgin Mother, but a close second is Mary Magdalene. Mary Magdalene was one of Jesus' contemporaries, one of his closest friends, and someone who spent much of his ministry by his side. She was reported to have been at his crucifixion as he died (many of the Apostles, exhausted from the events of previous few days, had left), and was one of the women to witness his empty tomb, and the first to whom he appeared after the Resurrection. For that brief time, before he appeared to the other apostles, she was the Church.

Debate the scientific and historical accuracy of Catholicism all you want, but her significance to Jesus' adult life as told in the gospels is hard to discount. Catholic scholars frequently compare the stories of the New Testament to each other, noting details shared across all four books, and those told only in a few. Mary's presence at the empty tomb is reported in all four.

Over the years, the roles for women in the Church have expanded, mostly to keep pace with the growth of the Church in developing nations relative to the decline in men entering the priesthood. It is worth mentioning that several Christian faiths have evolved to ordain women, but the Catholic Church deems itself the "true faith" as Jesus saw it, without derivation or modification to accommodate modernity since inception.

The Catholic Church has always exalted mothers; however, the predominant roles for religious women were as celibate nuns, or sisters, who served within the community as teachers, social workers, and nurses. Their role in the Church has never been equal to that of priests, nor have they been allowed by the Church to marry and bear children.

Historically, while women have not held formal positions of power and influence, they have contributed to and sacrificed for the Church. While there are only 784 female saints (canonized and recognized by Rome) of the over 10,000 total saints named since the inception of the Church, their stories contribute to the narrative of the Church and the role of women throughout the life of the institution. Conversely, 30 percent of all popes are now saints.

Perhaps the most iconoclastic of the female saints, Joan of Arc lived in France during the early 1400s. She believed that she heard voices of the Archangel Michael (and others) urging her to go to France to fight on behalf of France against the English in the Hundred Years' War. Historians are unclear as to her level of participation in the war, but military leaders are on record stating that they took her strategic advice, believing it to be divine. After leading a series of successful battles that eventually led to French victory, she was captured, tried by the English for heresy (including a charge of cross-dressing, which she did out of necessity and safety during battle), and burned at the stake at 19 years old. She later was posthumously declared innocent and a martyr, and beatified in 1909. To this day, she stands as a powerful representation of strength, conviction, and commitment for Catholics and non-Catholics.

Catherine of Siena lived in Italy in the late 1300s and rose to prominence in politics, brokering agreements between Pope Gregory and the leaders of secular Rome. Though she remained a layperson throughout her life, she established herself as a trusted advisor to the Vatican during a time of deep division between the states of Italy and the Holy See (the governmental jurisdiction of the Vatican). Her courage, forthrightness, and determination to preserve the Church were remarkable for a woman at that time. Her writings, including close to 400 letters, remain important historical documents. She was canonized in 1461, and in 1970, Pope Paul VI named her and St. Teresa of Avila Doctors of the Church, the first women to receive this honor, given to those who have contributed significantly to theology or Church doctrine.

The legacy of an American saint, Katharine Drexel, continues to advance the lives of those she helped while she was alive. Born in 1858 in Philadelphia to a wealthy and altruistic family, Drexel chose to enter the Sisters of Mercy, and would later use her inheritance to build boarding schools for Native Americans and African Americans. She founded her own religious order, Sisters of the Blessed Sacrament, to serve those communities, a mission to which it is still committed. During her lifetime, she established 50 schools for African American children and a dozen for Native Americans. It is estimated that she gave away close to $20 million over her lifetime.

Xavier University in New Orleans was founded by Katharine Drexel as an institute of higher learning for African Americans and is the first, and only, of the historically black colleges and universities founded by Catholics.

Drexel's devotion to underserved communities was not always appreciated. In 1913, Georgia tried to pass a law to prevent white teachers from teaching black students (the same law had been passed in neighboring Florida, and three white nuns had been arrested for violating it). Responding to a letter from the Ku Klux Klan threatening a pastor at one of her schools, the sisters prayed. Within a few days, the KKK headquarters was destroyed by a tornado, and two of their members were killed.

There were no more threats to the sisters or their schools after that.

I am voracious alone.

—*Brenda Shaughnessy*, "Postfeminism"

The Church has a long way to go to regain the trust of its followers and the faithful. Kerry Robinson's hope is to help heal the Church from the inside, but with the strong influence from laypeople who care deeply for the body of the Church. The only way this can happen is through elevation of women, giving their voices equal stature, and remembering how Jesus revered and trusted the women in his life.

Maria Giese

"*The absence of women directors in Hollywood
was tantamount to the silencing and censoring
of women's voices everywhere.*"

Hollywood has never been a welcoming place for women, regardless of their age, talent, or ethnicity. We're hearing lately, and loudly, from women about the power imbalances that led to widespread sexual abuse and assault, and the silence necessary to maintain a career. Men created Hollywood, and men continue to fund and produce much of what we consume. This is probably why writers' rooms are predominantly men, interesting characters are mostly men, and storylines revolve around topics relatable to men.

It is astounding to consider how much of our social and historical narrative has been written and influenced by rooms of white men. How many stories have been lost, untold, or changed to suit that narrative, the one that centers on men? So much of what we internalize about ourselves, our place in the world, the acceptable places for us to enter, start from what we see in film and on television. And when that perception is framed through only one lens, it stunts so many possibilities for so many of us.

If you play-act at butchery long enough you
grow used to the sounds of the screaming.
—*Brenna Twohy*, "Fantastic Breasts and
Where to Find Them"

The Directors Guild of America (DGA) was formed in the 1930s to represent directors and those on their teams in film, television, commercials, and new media. It exists to represent the creative and economic rights of directors and their teams. Among the benefits offered to members is a pension and health care retirement plan, something in which those who freelance rarely can participate. Hollywood, more than any other industry, relies heavily on the availability and economic model of freelancing. The DGA currently represents over 15,000 directors, 13.7 percent of whom are women.

Between 1939 and 1979, only 14 of the 7,332 films produced in the United States were directed by women. In response, six women in the DGA—the Original Six, as they became known—launched a campaign to expose the underrepresentation of women directors, which in 1979 was 0.5 percent. Their pursuit was certainly driven by wanting more women to influence the industry—but it was also financial. The pension and health care retirement benefit was awarded based on points that would accrue based on how many projects a member of the DGA had worked. Fewer women directors meant fewer points being assigned to women, which led to lower retirement benefits. Beyond getting the work, there was real money attached to this pursuit.

Michael Franklin was the National Executive Secretary of the DGA in 1979, the highest position within the organization, and the one with the most power. When the Original Six shared with him their findings, he vowed to do something. They encouraged movie studios and production companies to consider women for various roles but, because participation was voluntary and there were no penalties, results were abysmal. Franklin initiated legal action, and the DGA sued on behalf of their women and minority members.

In 1983, their work led to a class-action lawsuit against Warner Brothers and Columbia Pictures that was dismissed in 1985. Since the DGA stipulated that directors could hire their own assistant directors, the studios felt they could not be held responsible for discriminatory hiring practices, and filed a counterclaim. The female judge ruled, correctly, in favor of the studios, stating that there was a conflict of interest, but that the suit had merit. Had the women and minority directors been able to finance their own suit, they may have won.

The case was dropped for lack of financing, resulting in long-lasting effects on women in the craft—both in getting hired and accruing points toward their retirement.

The number of women in director roles steadily increased in the years following the attention from the Original Six, but peaked in 1995 and plateaued or decreased every year following.[33] This was mostly because when the Original Six brought their complaint to the DGA, the civil rights and feminist movements were still topics about which people were active and aware. By the '90s, feminism had lost much of its galvanizing power, as many women and their allies had become complacent. The DGA didn't elect their first female president of the association until 2002.

In 1995, women directed only 16 percent of television. The number of women with director credits hovers around 4 percent

---

[33]Women in the World Staff.

now, many of whom are stars themselves or related to powerful Hollywood men, distorting the path to power that is unavailable to most women. Between 2007 and 2016, 80 percent of female film directors made only one movie.

The Hurt Locker was released in 2009, and Kathryn Bigelow won the Oscar for Best Director that year. She was the first woman to ever win the award, and in that same year women directed only 7 percent of the top 250 domestic grossing films. Only five women have ever been nominated for Best Director, all have been white, and Bigelow is the only winner. (Six African American directors have been nominated for the Best Director Oscar, all are male, and none have won.)

Half of the kingdom is already gone

—*Countess of Winchilsea Anne Finch*, "The Introduction"

After successfully directing a few award-winning films, Maria Giese wasn't getting hired.

She knows she is one of many women who could have continued to create popular, award-winning films, if only she'd been given more chances. She wrote and directed *When Saturday Comes* then *Hunger*, which won Best Underground Feature at the 2007 FAIF festival and two Best Film Awards. Giese's work has won two CINE Golden Eagles, a Kovler Writing Award, a Spotlight Award, First Prize at the American International Film Festival, a

Charles Speroni Scholarship, and an MPAA Award of Excellence. Early in her career, after the release of *When Saturday Comes*, she signed with the William Morris Agency (WMA) and was attached to dozens of films but got pushed out of each of them. Then she got dropped by WMA.

Of the top 1,000 grossing films from 2007 to 2016, researchers from USC Annenberg found that 80 percent of women made only one film, but the number drops to 55 percent of men making only one film. On the other hand, Tyler Perry throws the number off for black male directors, as he was behind 25 percent of all the films made by black men.[34]

Giese started talking with other women directors and studying women's representation behind the camera. In 2013, she also launched the first (and as yet, only) Women's Summit for the members of the DGA, to strengthen the bonds among women directors, to amplify their voice to the broader DGA members, and to lead to more director jobs for women. A similar summit had been organized in 1999 by director Allison Anders, which built strong connections among women in ways that sustain into today, but with no tangible impact on the industry. Wanting a more lasting outcome, it was shortly after the 2013 summit that Giese decided to take her research to the ACLU, put her directing career on hold, and become a full-time activist.

---

something has tried to kill me and has failed
—*Lucille Clifton*, "won't you celebrate with me"

---

[34]Sun.

Under Dr. Stacy Smith, Founder and Director of the Annenberg Inclusion Initiative, which studies the impact of inequality in entertainment, the University of Southern California in 2016 published the Comprehensive Annenberg Report on Diversity in Entertainment (CARD). In it, the researchers ranked production companies and networks on their diversity at every level, both inside and onscreen. The findings are dramatic, both over time and as a reflection of where the industry is currently. Geena Davis, the Academy Award winning actress and founder of the Geena Davis Institute on Gender in Media, was one of the sponsors for the series of studies, four in total.

The 2016 study covered 414 total "stories" (109 motion pictures, 305 broadcast, cable, and digital series) released from 2014 to 2015. Their methodology covered minimum box office draw, definitions of speaking parts and major characters, and roles for those behind the camera.

Men onscreen outnumbered women 2:1, and women had less than 30 percent of all speaking roles in film. More men than women held lead roles in film (~75 percent). Interestingly, as streaming takes hold of the home viewing market, gender is leveling out with the highest percentage (44 percent) of women in lead roles.

Only 35 percent of all characters evaluated in this study were over 40 years old, and of those, about 75 percent were men. Variances across media show fewer roles for women over 40 cast in film than any other platform.

The area where women have the highest percentage of representation, not surprisingly, is sexualization. Across all media, women were also shown partially naked in 33 percent of the sample, while men were only in 10 percent.

The writer Alison Bechdel, the playwright behind the brilliant, semi-autobiographical memoir and Tony-winning musical

Fun Home, in 1985 created the Bechdel Test, which challenges roles for women to be multidimensional. Bechdel was loosely inspired by Virginia Woolf's *A Rooms of One's Own*, which may be the first published work to meaningfully critique female characters as being limited to the role they play in relation to others—wife, mother, or other.

The Bechdel Test's requirements:

1. The movie has to have at least two women in it,
2. who talk to each other,
3. about something besides a man.

Think about your favorite film and see how it rates against those three simple criteria. It's harder if the film was pre-2010, but still challenging for the majority of Hollywood output. Comic book writer Kelly Sue DeConnick has suggested what she calls the sexy lamp test: "If you can take a female character out and replace her with a sexy lamp and your plot still functions, you're a hack."[35]

The Directors Guild of America has only recently (since 2009) begun studying and publishing reports on diversity. Their findings are not surprising, showing that the majority of directors are still overwhelmingly white and male, but the number of women and people of color are increasing. Streaming television has shaken the tree significantly, introducing not only new ways to consume entertainment, but new topics and teams in front of and behind the cameras—a very encouraging trend.

The 2018 success of both *Black Panther* and *Crazy Rich Asians* has proven the market is ripe for strong ethnic casts and storylines. The last feature film with an all-Asian cast was *Joy Luck Club* in 1993. *Black Panther*, created in print in 1966 by Marvel Comics

---

[35]Nick U., "DeConnick."

to attract black fans, features a strong black African male lead in Wakanda, an isolated African country full of technological and scientific wonders, and also full of strong black women. Too often, the stories told with all or predominantly black casts are those of suffering and struggle, or rely on a White Savior to change the narrative. *Black Panther* is none of those.

Ava DuVernay, director of *Selma,* and *13th,* is also the creative force behind *Queen Sugar,* which is now in its fourth season on the Oprah Winfrey network. She has committed to an all-female directorial staff. *New York Times* film critic Manohla Dargis suggested the DuVernay Test, while discussing the 2016 Nate Parker film *Birth of a Nation* about the slave-led revolt of 1831. As she states, for a film to pass the DuVernay test, it is one "in which African Americans and other minorities have fully realized lives rather than serve as scenery in white stories."[36]

These observations are important, because they bring to light the lack of representation in an industry that powerfully shapes our world views, our self-perceptions, and our ability to see our place in the world. When mostly white men create, produce, and star in the stories, our value is formed relative to them. And that takes time and self-awareness to undo.

Shrinking don't come easy to us giants.

—Jessica Greyhaus, "Heels"

---

[36]Dargis.

Another segment of the population that is grossly underrepresented are people with disabilities. And when they are represented, it's often through the lens of a single dimension, without the complexity and depth of personality given to other characters.

Stacy Lawrence is a filmmaker and she also happens to be deaf. She's been a friend of mine since we went to high school together in the '80s at a midsize Catholic high school in suburban Connecticut. She was the only deaf person in our high school, and the only deaf person in her large Italian family.

Her mother introduced her to art at an early age, which developed into a passion for photography. She had planned to major in photography at the Rochester Institute of Technology, but her mother died unexpectedly when we were in high school, and the camera became a painful reminder of that connection. It wasn't until more than a decade later, when she was about to go into labor with her first child and purchased a brand-new camera, that her love for film was reborn.

Many of her most vivid memories are trips to movie theaters with family who took turns interpreting films using informal, self-created sign language. Captioning was not widely available in the early '70s, so Lawrence was left to figure out what specific facial expressions and body language meant, and her brain was always filling up with visual details about each object just to help her understand each scene.

When her parents tried to sign her up for local photography and film classes, they learned that interpreters were not provided, making it impossible for her to participate.

Years later, when she easily registered her two hearing children for similar classes, she remembered her own experience with the barriers to full access to smooth communication. At first, she assumed that opportunities for deaf children had improved. It was the early 2000s, long after the advent of captioning and the passing of the Americans with Disabilities Act. And American Sign Language's cinematic value and impact on mainstream culture couldn't be denied after Marlee Matlin won the 1986 Academy Award for Best Actress in *Children of a Lesser God*. But Lawrence assumed wrong.

As a result, she founded Deaf Film Camp, the first program for deaf and hard-of-hearing students to learn filmmaking without barriers. She hired highly qualified deaf filmmakers from all corners of the world to communicate with the campers in sign language. She started it as an overnight camp in upstate New York, but due to the strong feedback to her viral "HAPPY" music video in the summer of 2014, Deaf Film Camp became increasingly popular. Many teenagers wanted to attend, and deserved access to a language-enriched environment, so she changed the business model. Now she drops into high schools—both hearing and deaf schools—and immerses herself and her program in their world for a week.

She credits Marilyn Willrich and Nikki Stratton as early mentors in showing her that running a business that focuses on deaf clients and consumers can not only be successful, but can also be contagious. They launched the United Kingdom's leading film and arts festival, showcasing the work of deaf artists and filmmakers from all over the world.

The teenagers with whom Lawrence works closely thrive while exploring the general art of filmmaking. But now they have a new way to communicate their ideas: a medium that was not always available to their predecessors. They understand that they need to help both hearing and deaf individuals to understand that access to films is a multilayered proposition, requiring accurate captioning and interpreters. It is also essential that interpreters are knowledgeable about the technical aspects of film production, particularly when meeting potential investors to raise funds for film projects, but also to interpret filming language at filming sets, voice over at booths, music and background sounds on film, and explaining how editing software programs work in terms of audio.

they shone so by moonlight that the sows stampeded
—*Carolyn Kizer*, "Semele Recycled"

F inding and building a pipeline of talent is not the problem. Women currently make up half of all major film school graduates, when only 10 years ago they were about a third.[37] Anecdotal analysis shows that women are simply not trusted with the same budgets given to men for films. The studios, still largely run by men, do not want to risk hiring women. The current success formula works for them, and they do not want to change that. In this way, Hollywood is exactly like every other industry I studied for this book.

Since 2003, the Tisch School of the Arts at New York University has hosted an annual film festival under the guidance of Susan Sandler, a Golden Globe nominated screenwriter. The Fusion Film Festival showcases women's work and women's technical talent. Sandler bristles against the assumption that women only tell women's stories, since men have been telling women's stories all along (albeit not always accurately).

---

[37]Murphy.

Alice Guy-Blaché is credited with being the first female director, including the first narrative film *The Cabbage Fairy*, and participated in the production of 1,000 films from 1896 through about 1920. Before 1925, just about half of all films were written by women. When films included soundtracks, and studios became big businesses, Wall Street investors got involved and men took over.

Guy-Blaché's films often featured women in strong, independent roles, and she portrayed marriage as an equal partnership. Guy-Blaché made a film about Planned Parenthood in the early 1900s, and *A Fool and His Money*, the first film featuring an all African American cast. (Originally, it was going to have a mixed cast but the white actors quit when they learned they'd split screen time with blacks).

She built her own film studio in Fort Lee, New Jersey, the largest at the time, which became a hub for filming until the industry moved to Los Angeles around 1919. She died in 1968, after lecturing for years and trying to correct the historical record of the film industry that had largely written her out. In 2012, the DGA presented her posthumously the Lifetime Achievement Award. A documentary about her life, *Be Natural: The Untold Story of Alice Guy-Blaché* written, edited, produced, and directed by Pamela B. Green with executive producer Robert Redford, screened at IFC Cannes and Telluride in 2018, and was released in theaters in 2019.

Norman Lear, the famous writer and producer of many groundbreaking television series in the 1970s, such as *All In The Family* and *The Jeffersons*, was an early advocate for women on and behind the screen—but with limitations. He has been quoted as saying, "the kind of strength needed to direct has nothing to do with brute force, it has to do with strength of character,"[38] but

---

[38]Mills.

he never changed anything at any of his companies with regard to hiring more women, even after participating in meetings with the Original Six, and reportedly being moved by their research and passion. Lear changed forever the television sitcom when he introduced characters who spoke about politics, race, and feminism, topics no other television series dared to discuss, so it's not as though he feared being controversial. The caricatural depictions of various characters has been criticized over the years, but his impact on the modern sitcom cannot be dismissed. It's hard not to imagine the impact he could have made had he chosen to support the movement started by the Original Six.

Lucille Ball, star of *I Love Lucy* in the '50s, was the first female head of a production company—DesiLu. It was founded with her husband Desi Arnaz, and run by her alone after their divorce when she bought him out. Their show was one of the first to portray a mixed-ethnicity couple, and it only came about because she insisted on it. When the show became a huge hit, syndication made them the first television millionaires.

Ball's pregnancy was one of the first ever shown and discussed openly on network television, although the word "pregnant" didn't pass the censors, so she was "expecting." Each episode was screened for a priest, rabbi, and minister so as not to offend. The precautions must have worked, because more households tuned in for Little Ricky's arrival in January of 1953 than for President Eisenhower's inauguration the following day.

One of Ball's top writers, and her only female writer, was Madelyn Pugh Davis, whose career was launched at CBS radio during World War II when male writers were scarce. She was the second woman writer ever hired at CBS, and officially, her title was "Girl Writer." Her original aspiration upon graduating from Indiana University was to be a foreign correspondent, but, as she writes in her autobiography, "Somebody pointed out that there were very few women foreign correspondents, but there were very few women anything, so it didn't bother me." Her style and wit secured Ball's stardom, and Ball lavished praise on her writers whenever possible. In addition to writing the lines and the physical stunts for Ball's character, Davis would often be the first to act them out for plausibility before turning them over to the cast members.

The Paley Center for Media honored her in 2006: "During the formative years of television, when few women were working behind the screen, Madelyn Pugh Davis wrote one of the most popular shows of all time. She not only made her mark as a writer, but also opened the door for other women to follow in her footsteps."

In 1973, CBS named Ethel Winant vice president, making her the first female executive at that network, but also the first female TV executive in history. (CBS didn't offer her any bump in pay for the promotion, but she successfully argued for "a little more money."[39]) When they moved her office to the executive floor, there was no women's restroom. Winant learned to leave her high heels outside the men's room door to let her colleagues know she was in there, as supposedly there was also no lock on the door.

A woman like that is not ashamed to die.

—*Anne Sexton*, "Her Kind"

---

[39]Gregory.

Sophia Vergara, the Columbian actress most of us know from her role on the ABC sitcom *Modern Family*, might not be the first person who comes to mind as a champion for other women. Her character, Gloria, is beautiful, is married to a much older wealthy man, and has a thick accent that distracts only slightly from her tight wardrobe. It's easy to discount the actress based on the role, and she's happy to let you do that. But don't.

Forbes calls her the highest paid TV actress, but her wealth comes only partially from her TV credits. In 2017, she made $41.5 million, slightly below her 2016 $43 million, and she has topped the *Forbes* list since 2010. The majority of her earnings come from endorsements and management of other actors.

Back in 1998, Vergara landed her first endorsement for Bally Fitness. It ran in Spanish (most ads back then were overdubbed rather than filmed in Spanish) and it resonated with the Spanish-speaking market. She was one of the first Latin actors to endorse a product to the US market.

Hispanic buying power in the United States is currently estimated at $1.3 trillion according to the Selig Center for Economic Growth,[40] and is expected to be $1.7 trillion by 2020. With growth outpacing any other segment, Hispanics are the largest minority group in the United States at 18 percent of the population. Even when lower immigration and birth rates are factored, Nielsen projects Hispanics to be 24 percent of the United States by 2040, and 29 percent by 2060.[41]

Average household income has also steadily increased for Hispanic homes, according to the US Census Bureau, from just over $40,000 in 2009 to just over $42,000 in 2014, and Hispanic

---

[40]Humphreys.
[41]Nielsen.

households with a total income higher than $50,000 rose from 30 percent in 2000 to 43 percent in 2014.[42]

Vergara and her business partner, Luis Balaguer, saw that not only was the Latin market not being tapped, but Latin actors were not well represented. They founded Latin World Entertainment (LatinWE) in 1994 to consult with brands on how best to reach the Latin market, and provide skilled experience to represent Latin actors who were not accustomed to negotiating with large studios and powerful executives. They worked with movie studios to market films to Hispanic audiences.

The firm is 100 percent Hispanic owned. And since its founding, it's grown to be the premier multimedia marketing, production, licensing agency for Latino actors and brands wishing to reach Latino audiences.

At a time when Latin actors were negotiating their own contracts—without lawyers or agents to navigate an unfamiliar landscape in, for many, an unfamiliar language—Latin World Entertainment provided a trusted partner. It was the first and is now the largest talent management agency for Latin actors. In addition to TV and film roles, LatinWE also works with brands to match Hispanic stars with products—key to targeting a new and growing market of buyers.

Growing the largest Latin talent agency before the United States saw the potential of the Latin market was a prescient move by Vergara and the team at LatinWE. But the impact LatinWE has had on the actors it represents is extraordinary.

Vergara and her team have gradually made Latin culture more mainstream and, in doing so, have shaken long held stereotypes. She is frequently criticized for capitalizing on such stereotypes through her character on *Modern Family*, but she doesn't care. That one of

---

[42]Ibid.

the most popular, most highly paid prime time actresses is a thickly accented Latina, appeals to a wide audience and has a well-developed character is a significant achievement.

In 2017, Norman Lear and Netflix brought back *One Day at a Time*, a popular sitcom from the '70s. But this time, the cast centered on a Cuban family—the women in particular—much in the same way the original series focused on the women in the Romano/ Cooper family. In its first year, the revamped series was named one of the top shows of the year and received wide critical acclaim and Emmy nominations—which made Netflix's decision in early 2019 to cancel the show a devastating blow to its creators, stars, and fans. Rumors that Norman Lear met with Netflix's head of content to reconsider the cancellation and that several threads on social media pleaded with the company to release them from their contractual obligations in order to be picked up by another network, seemed to have had an impact, but the outcome is as yet unknown.

---

a caged bird stands on the grave of dreams
—*Maya Angelou*, "Caged Bird"

In 2013, after the Women of Action Summit for the DGA members, Maria Giese presented her research work on behalf of women directors to the ACLU, and several of their senior attorneys launched a media and advocacy campaign that would last two years. It included a letter to the Equal Employment Opportunity

Commission (EEOC) calling for an industry-wide investigation, which was also published by the *New York Times*.[43] The EEOC is a division of the Federal Department of Justice, founded in 1964 as part of the Civil Rights Act to enforce Title VII, which prohibits discrimination in every aspect of employment.

In late 2015, the EEOC launched the biggest investigation into the film industry's discrimination against women, specifically women directors. It remains the only investigation that the EEOC has made into Hollywood's discrimination against women.

One of the challenges with upholding the Title VII legislation is that it only applies to employers with more than 15 employees, and many people working in entertainment work as contractors. And a particularly problematic part of the DGA contract is that its diversity requirement includes anyone who is not a white man. Because of this, many of the jobs are filled by nonwhite men, the box is checked, and women are still left out.

In 2016, it was reported that all six major studios were in violation of discriminating against women, and settlement talks with Federal Government had begun.[44] Outcomes are still unknown because the EEOC does not comment on ongoing investigations or settlement discussions. Charges are only made public if a lawsuit is filed, which has not happened yet in this case.

The timing of all of this, dovetailing with the massive outpouring of stories of sexual assault and harassment by many of the most influential and powerful in Hollywood, could influence the industry in a number of divergent directions. One is that it will provide further credentials to the stories of the accusers, demonstrating their lack of influence and forced subjugation to the men in power. It could also push women farther back from power, as the backlash

---

[43]Buckley.
[44]Robb.

in Hollywood is legendary and the financing of films and television is controlled by very few. It could inspire an entirely new structure for hiring filmmakers, if the decisions by the large studios are more closely reported. Actors could enforce the Inclusion Rider, which requires the studios to hire a defined number of women, minorities, disabled, and LGBTQ for each production, wielding their power for the benefit of others.

Recently, Procter & Gamble, the largest advertiser in the United States with $7 billion in ad spend in 2017 alone, pledged to have half of their commercials directed by women by 2023. Looking back at the response to their "Better Man" ad, and the conversations it sparked on both sides of the toxic masculinity debate, I can't wait to see what they create.

The work Giese is doing to hold accountable the major film studios, the DGA, and the film industry is changing the systems and structures of Hollywood and will create the lasting, sustainable change from the inside. The root of systemic sexual harassment is the imbalance of power, and that imbalance is predicated on who controls the money. Without equal protections under the law, and without regulations that end these practices, women will have fewer places than they currently do, largely due to the fear men now have about working with and around women.

One thing that has dramatically changed for women: we are being heard. For the first time, women in Hollywood, across a number of disciplines, are heard, believed, and supported.

Cindy Gallop

"Women challenge the status quo because we are never it.**"** [45]

C indy Gallop is best known for disrupting the advertising industry. She challenges the space to get better—to have more women executives, to represent women multidimensionally in their work, and to make room for women and people of color across all aspects of the business of advertising.

And now she's out to forever change the way we talk about and think about sex, sexuality, and women's right to pleasure. Gallop's social sex startup MakeLoveNotPorn aims to provide a platform to foster open, honest communication around real sex between real people, and replace the erroneous transactional sex depicted in most easily accessible online pornography.

Pain is no stronger than the resisting force
—*Mina Loy*, "Partuition"

---

[45]Chandelier Creative.

E veryone remembers the first time they saw pornography. If we consider pornography to mean the visual depiction of the act of sex, then we can also recognize that such images were recorded with the earliest parietal art discovered in caves. The most natural of behaviors, the one act from which the species relies for survival, has inflamed debates for centuries.

Men control the lifespan of pornography. They profit from it and legislate against it. They consume it, they produce it, they distribute it. The lens through which most pornography is created is the male perspective. Women are ridiculously proportioned, storylines are predictable and shallow, and the sex is centered around male ejaculation and gratification.

But inasmuch as society and the legal system have tried to squelch and suppress access to sexual content, it has found its way into every media; oftentimes leading innovation for those forms. There are differing opinions on the legitimacy of this, but legend states that when in-home video first hit the market in the late '70s, two competing technologies vied for market dominance: VHS and Betamax. Betamax offered superior image quality, but was only able to hold an hour of video. VHS allowed three hours of continuous play, albeit with lower image quality, appealing to the in-home pornography viewer who liked not having to change the tape but every three hours. Sales of VHS players quickly outpaced Betamax, and by the end of the '70s, erotic film sales were half of all VHS tape sales in the United States.[46]

Even the first electronic payment systems were born from pornography. When 900 numbers were popular—a fee-based phone number providing updates on anything from sports scores to crossword puzzle answers, but most notably for adult chat lines—the banks didn't want to process the payments, mainly because so

---

[46]Glass.

many were contested when an unsuspecting partner questioned the charge, thinking their chaste spouse would never have made such a call. And credit card companies hadn't yet learned how to secure payments that weren't made in person.

Seeing an open market, Richard Gordon, a former insurance salesman and finance planner who had been convicted of fraud and served two years in prison, launched a business that processed payments for 900 numbers and infomercials for a percentage of each charge. When a supposedly stolen video of drummer Tommy Lee and model Pamela Anderson having sex in 1995 was made available as a pay-per-view Internet download—the first celebrity video of its kind to do so—Gordon's business processed all of the payments.

The biggest inhibitors for the online porn business are devices and platforms. Both are controlled largely by Google, Apple, Facebook, YouTube, and Amazon, and each have prevented the proliferation of pornography videos and apps through their devices or on their platforms, for very good reasons of controlling access to minors. This has also slowed the creation of new technologies, a place where pornography used to lead.

Access to fresh content, and privacy in which to view it, are two factors in pornography consumption. Affordable personal video recorders and viewing devices allowed everyone to create and enjoy pornography in their living rooms and bedrooms. During the nascent days of the Internet, modems couldn't handle video file sizes, but plenty of images were shared across bulletin board forums. In 1996, of the 10 most popular Usenet forums (early low bandwidth Internet forums), half were adult-content oriented.

"Mr. President, Georgetown University Law School has released a remarkable study conducted by researchers at Carnegie Mellon University. ... The university surveyed 900,000 computer images. Of these 900,000 images,

> 83.5 percent of all computerized photographs available on the Internet are pornographic. Mr. President, I want to repeat that: 83.5 percent of the 900,000 images reviewed—these are all on the Internet—are pornographic, according to the Carnegie Mellon study."
>
> *—Senator Charles Grassley (Rep. Iowa),*
> June 26, 1995[47]

The Communications Decency Act, signed into law in 1996 by President Bill Clinton, was the first attempt by Congress to regulate content on the newly commercialized Internet. First Amendment rights have stood firm against the right to create and sell pornography. But our legislation, owing as much to the advanced age and lack of technology familiarity of our legislators, has greatly lagged advancements in technology in many more critical areas beyond the distribution of legal pornography.

In 2001, there were 70,000 adult websites and, in 2017, there were over four million in the United States alone, with an estimated 30 million porn viewers every second. Popular aggregator sites such as Facebook and YouTube claim to not allow adult content on their pages, but content creators have always found ways to circumvent filters.

The social impact of such easy access to all varieties of pornography has yet to be truly understood. Early indicators show that middle school children cannot fully grasp what they watch, and their understanding of intimate relationships is skewed. Without factual conversations with adults, misconceptions about partnering and roles become ingrained.

A large survey of American young people revealed that 51 percent of males and 32 percent of females claimed to have

---

[47]Klotz.

viewed pornography for the first time before they were 13 years old.[48] Early and repeated pornography consumption by young men leads to increasingly callous responses to women, acceptance of rape mythology as fact, and increased proclivity toward deviant and violent forms of sexual expression.[49]

Perhaps the most fascinating finding from this study: women who watched pornography regularly beginning at a young (pre-teen) age did not want to someday have daughters.

In a 2014 survey on pornography consumption by American adults, 79 percent of 18-30-year-old males reported viewing pornography at least once per month, with 63 percent more than once per week. For women of the same age, 34 percent viewed it once per month, and only 19 percent more than once per week.[50] When society shames sex and does not include sex education in science and biology curricula and adolescents' natural curiosity can only be sated through Internet searches, perceptions of what are normal, healthy sexual interactions are warped. In Cindy Gallop's words, "hardcore pornography has become de facto sex education."

And young men are responding strongly to a never-ending supply of fresh, readily available two-dimensional stimulus, at the expense of developing intimate relationships with living, breathing three-dimensional humans. Gary Wilson, known for his TED Talk on the effects of pornography on the brain, believes foundationally in the Coolidge Effect. This is when males of a species have a quicker sexual response and higher levels of dopamine with new female partners than with the same female partner. He applies this to pornography in that there is a constant supply of new material, often leading to increased levels of erectile dysfunction in younger

---

[48]Leahy.

[49]Minarcik, Wetterneck, and Short.

[50]American College of Pediatricians.

and younger men, negatively altering their stimulus response in encounters with real partners.

What would happen if one woman
told the truth about her life?
The world would split open.

—*Muriel Rukeyser*, "Käthe Kollwitz"

But what if there was a counterpoint to pornography, one that depicted love, real bodies, and true intimacy in much the same way that we observe and consume other connections between humans through social media platforms? What if our revulsion talking about sex could evolve through such socialization toward accepting sex as important, healthy, and natural?

Cindy Gallop wants to make it easier for the world to talk openly and factually about sex.

She launched MakeLoveNotPorn in 2009 to do just that. Her goal is to accurately celebrate how real people have real sex, something no one else is doing. She wants to share how funny, messy, beautiful, awkward, and human sex can be. MakeLoveNotPorn is the first social sex video-sharing platform, one built on a revenue-sharing business model. Members pay a subscription that allows them to rent and view videos on the site, and half of the income goes to the MakeLoveNotPornstars, those who create and contribute their content to the site. Curators at MakeLoveNotPorn guarantee adherence to the community guidelines of authentic, consensual, cliché-free content. MakeLoveNotPorn's videos celebrate real-world bodies, real-world sex, real-world emotions—love, intimacy, feelings.

Nowhere else is the distribution of power more clear than in sex. While men are also victims of sexual assault and women have committed sexual assault, overwhelmingly, it is women who are assaulted by men. It is estimated that every 98 seconds, an American is sexually assaulted, and one in six American women experienced rape or attempted rape in her lifetime.[51]

And we're not helping our boys grow into men capable of building true partnerships with women if most of the imagery they see and the language they hear is of subservient women. When we assign strength, power, control, and success to men, and supportive, nurturing, deferential roles to women, children internalize those traits and it becomes difficult to rewrite those narratives. When we encourage our daughters to exhibit masculine traits, but don't equally encourage our sons to display feminine traits, we force them into narrowly defined roles, which often constrain and limit their development into their authentic selves.

Sex education in schools is highly politicized, resulting in wide variations and inconsistencies state to state, and private schools are left to their own to devise curriculum. In my small Catholic school, we were never taught the biology of sex, only the moral obligation not to have it within the context of the Ten Commandments. But we were never taught what exactly it was we were not supposed to have. As a child, I believed that women just grew babies when they reached a certain age, in the same way they grew breasts or hair in certain places, or grew taller. I realized there might be something else involved after one of our school nuns spoke with us about "being called" to the priesthood or convent and I asked, earnestly, what

---

[51]RAINN.

happened if a nun had a baby, and I was sent to the principal's office. That was definitely not the time or place to ask any more questions.

Under President Ronald Reagan, abstinence-only sex education—teaching kids to wait until they are in a committed, monogamous, heterosexual marriage to have sex—qualified for federal funding. Between 1996 and 2010, over $1.5 billion has been spent on abstinence-only programs, with questionable efficacy.

As of 2017:

- ❖ 22 states and the District of Columbia require public schools to teach sex education, 20 of which require contraceptive and HIV education.
- ❖ 33 states and the District of Columbia require students to receive HIV/AIDS instruction.
- ❖ 19 states require that, if provided, sex education must be medically, factually, or technically accurate.
- ❖ 18 states and the District of Columbia require that information on contraception be provided.
- ❖ 37 states require that information on abstinence be provided, 12 of which require that abstinence be stressed.
- ❖ 19 states require that instruction on the importance of engaging in sexual activity only within marriage be provided.
- ❖ 13 states require the inclusion of information on the negative outcomes of teen sex and pregnancy.[52]
- ❖ 38 states and the District of Columbia require school districts to allow parental involvement in sexual education programs.
- ❖ Four states require parental consent before a child can receive instruction.

---

[52]FindLaw.

❖ 35 states and the District of Columbia allow parents to opt-out on behalf of their children.[53]

In 2014, fewer than half of high schools and only 20 percent of middle schools provided instruction on all 16 topics that the Centers for Disease Control and Prevention (CDC) considers essential to sexual health education.[54] A 2011 survey from the CDC reports that 47 percent of all high school students have had sex and 15 percent of them have had sex with four or more partners. There is no way of knowing how many of them live in states that do not require medically or factually accurate sex education.

Sex education in public schools ranges from abstinence-only instruction to comprehensive discussions about birth control, STDs, LGBTQ education, and age of consent. With wide variances in parental involvement and permissions, hours dedicated to instruction, degrees to which subjects are taught, expertise of instructor, scientific versus religious focus, it's difficult to ascertain efficacy of any method. Numerous studies have and will always be conducted, with results either promoted or dismissed by whichever group they serve.

Of course, the best educators about sex, respect, self-esteem, and consent are families, but not every adolescent has that, and I believe as a society, we should provide safe places for kids with questions to get factual, nonjudgmental answers. For many, school is the only other place where they speak with adults every day.

What we're creating, without intention, is a broken relationship ideology that is equally affecting all of our young people. Those who do not have loving, healthy, adult relationships around them to model, and even some who do, struggle to process and internalize

---

[53]National Conference of State Legislators.
[54]Guttmacher Institute.

the deluge of imagery served to them and how to form lasting, respectful, and intimate relationships.

Sexuality is not something we encourage women to pursue or enjoy, even as adults in committed monogamous relationships. The expression of a woman's sexual pleasure is viewed as vulgar and reviled, by other women as often as men. We raise girls in a hyper-sexualized society but don't provide adequate education or context for them to develop a healthy understanding of their sexuality and how to express it.

Women's bodies have the only organ designed solely for plea-sure: the clitoris. Though small, it is dense with nerve endings, highly responsive to stimulation, and capable of eliciting female orgasm. A male penis has about 4,000 nerve endings, while a clitoris has about 8,000. The clitoris is not commonly discussed in sex education, nor is it widely covered in medical training. And yet it is the most erog-enous zone for either gender.

Some cultures still enforce female genital mutilation, which removes the external genitalia from girls at birth or through puberty and almost always removes the clitoris, sometimes also removing the inner and outer labia. The United Nations has denounced the prac-tice since 2010. There are no known health benefits to female genital mutilation.

Women's and men's experiences with sex are vastly different, in physical experience and perception of the experience. A recent sur-vey of men and women asked them to describe a sexual encounter on the low end of the satisfaction scale and the variance was star-tling: women talked about pain or negative emotional response; men never imagined harmful outcomes for themselves.[55]

---

[55]Loofbourow.

> when they were born with tigers breathing
> between their thighs
> —*Tishani Doshi*, "The River of Girls"

indy Gallop would love for her social sex site to generate and share as much revenue as YouTube stars do now. However, many funding sources—banks, payment processors, hosting, coding—won't work with adult content, forcing Gallop to create those systems for herself. She believes sextech is the biggest opportunity for massive positive social benefit, in that it can help normalize sex and dispel our insecurities and fears—and it's therefore set to be the next trillion-dollar category in tech.

Gallop is raising $2 million to scale MakeLoveNotPorn. But she's also raising $200 million to start the world's first and only sextech fund, All The Sky Holdings, primarily focused on funding sextech ventures founded by women, and funding building the sextech infrastructure and ecosystem to support it.

Each chapter in this book sets out to frame the ways in which women have had to adjust and accommodate to fit within the accepted structures of dress and conduct. There are very few spaces where women have agency to express themselves free from the judgment of others. Transforming the way we talk about and teach sex, biology, sexual expression, consent, and respect with regard to intimate relationships would create a radically different, and quite possibly much healthier and safer, world for everyone.

Gallop is hoping to give women a that kind of place. A place where they can not only share their own sex, but explore the ways others also experience sex, and share in the business profits as the sextech category grows.

Alyza Bohbot

"I wanted to ensure that these women would truly gain access to fair market distribution, financing, education, and resources."

Alyza Bohbot owns a coffee company in Minnesota. Her parents started Alakef Coffee Roasters in 1990, after moving to Duluth, Minnesota, and feeling a void in the premium coffee market. When they started to think about retiring, Bohbot moved back to Minnesota to consider keeping her parents' business in the family. She loved it, and her parents sold the business to her in 2014. The business was solid, profitable, but flat, and she knew if it was going to be successful under her leadership, she needed to make bold changes and take some chances. So, she launched City Girl Coffee in 2015, with a clear purpose. She wanted to build a brand focused on gender equality in the coffee business.

> If you had to wear my shoes, you'd probably
> take them off too
>
> —*Shea Diamond*, "I Am Her"

Coffee, tea, and wine are powerful and important elements in world history, but only coffee, which originated in what is now Yemen, was for centuries only consumed in community, never at home. From Yemen, it spread widely across Turkey and Iran, North Africa, and the Middle East. Italians and Greeks then adopted it, but maintained much of its original preparation—small, strong, dense drinks shared amid intellectual conversations.

Much as with wine, when production had to grow to meet market demand, other similar climates began harvesting coffee and creating their own modified flavor profiles. Now, coffee is grown in Africa, Asia, the Caribbean, Central and South America, with Brazil being the largest producer as of 2016.

Coffee is second only to crude oil as the most produced and traded commodity in the world, valued at $100 trillion globally.

The World Bank estimates that more than 500 million people globally depend on coffee for their livelihoods, and over 25 million of them are coffee farmers. Over 90 percent of the world's coffee production comes from the developing world.

Oxfam, the international NGO confederation, reports that in worldwide food production, women perform 66 percent of the work, produce 50 percent of the food, but earn only 10 percent of the income and own 1 percent of the property. And, in the coffee industry, a 2009 survey by the International Trade Forum showed that women perform 70 percent of the fieldwork and harvest, while owning only 20 percent of the land and 10 percent of the companies.[56] This is largely due to laws in many countries preventing women from owning land independently, limited education for women once they begin menstruating, and cultural traditions beyond their ability to control. Women rarely write legislation in many of the countries where coffee production is high, another factor that contributes to their inequality. Women are often burdened with farm and family obligations, leaving little room for them to participate in the operational aspects of the business, even if those opportunities are open to them.

City Girl Coffee sources all of their coffee from women-owned farms and cooperatives all over the world, with a portion of their profits reinvested back into those communities through organizations that support women in each country.

In October of 2014, while attending an annual breakfast for the International Women's Coffee Alliance (IWCA), Bohbot heard a story about a Colombian woman who owned a coffee farm with her husband. The conflict inside Colombia has raged for over 50 years, and many Colombian men have died as a result. After this Colombian woman's husband was killed fighting, she assumed ownership of their farm. When she needed to replace an expensive piece of farm equipment, she was unable to secure a loan simply because of her gender. Bohbot learned that this was much more common in Colombia and other agricultural economies than she had previously been aware. The IWCA was formed in 2003 to give voice to women in coffee through independently organized local groups that advocate for women's equality across the spectrum of the industry. The IWCA works to provide additional market opportunities for

---

[56]International Trade Forum.

women farmers and connects them with each other for learning and resource sharing.

---

you can't make homes out of human beings

—*Warsan Shire*, "for women who are 'difficult' to love"

The coffee supply chain is centuries old, and truly global. A writer, A.J. Jacobs, wrote a book and delivered a TED Talk called *Thanks a Thousand* where he tried to personally thank every person who contributed to his morning cup of coffee. It's an entertaining story, because every time he meets someone, they mention several other people who played a part. His biggest learning was the thousand things that have to go right every day for him to enjoy that one cup of coffee. He talks about the truckers, the construction crews that pave the roads, the team that creates the asphalt on the roads, the guy who designed the perfect lid for your coffee, with the arc that collects the evaporation to preserve the aroma and flavor, the clean water we in the United States take for granted that so many people all over the world do not have.

He leaves you thinking about gratitude, describing it as "taking a moment and holding onto it as long as possible," whether it's that cup of perfectly executed coffee, or whatever it may be. We need to see more clearly and extend a greater appreciation for those moments in our daily mundane lives.

Here in the United States, the preponderance of low-wage farmworkers is hiding in plain sight. Many of the people who harvest and work the farms that stock the shelves of our local groceries are exploited, underpaid, and expendable to their employers. Some estimates are that six out of every ten farmworkers in the United States are undocumented, and eight out of ten were not born in the United States.

It is estimated that three million migrant and seasonal farmworkers are in the United States, 700,000 of whom are women, each making between $10,000 and $12,500 per year. Women make significantly less than men and are subject to sexual harassment, discrimination, and abuse in the fields. Workers are breathing in pesticides (leading to skin, respiratory, and reproductive diseases) and suffering from heat exposure. The power structure is firmly on the side of the employer, leaving the migrant worker little recourse when abuses occur.

In the 1930s, the United States passed a number of laws to protect workers, most notably the Fair Labor Standards Act, which mandated a minimum wage and prohibited child labor and unpaid overtime. However, farmworkers and domestic laborers were excluded from these protections. It wasn't until 1966 that the law was amended to include farmworkers. (In 1986, the law changed so that the Secretary of Labor could issue certificates to businesses to allow them to pay wages lower than the minimum to workers whose productivity was negatively affected by age, physical or mental disability, or injury.)

After World War II, facing a labor shortage in the fields when factories were on the rise and paying much more than farmwork, the United States government and Mexico entered into an agreement to bring agricultural labor from Mexico to the United States, in lieu of drafting Mexican soldiers to fight with the Allies. Known as the Bracero Program, it brought as many as 445,000 workers to the

United States at its peak in 1956. Negotiated between the governments, workers were guaranteed a minimum wage, acceptable living conditions, protection from discrimination, and exemption from military service. The program was, however, riddled with abuses and unreported violations, with simultaneous annual increases in the number of workers illegally seeping into the United States, until in 1954 the US government started Operation Wetback, the appallingly-named organized deportation program that sent over one million immigrants back to Mexico in its first year, where they were relocated to the areas in Mexico that most needed laborers. The Bracero Program continued until December of 1964, when it was discontinued by Congress.

Then, on Cinco de Mayo in 1965, the US government launched a program to try to fill the labor gap with American students who needed summer jobs. The Secretary of Labor, Willard Wirtz, set out to recruit 20,000 high school athletes for the A-TEAM (Athletes in Temporary Employment as Agricultural Manpower) to work on the farms in California, earning money and staying in shape.

Working six days a week, starting each day at 6 a.m. to avoid the midday heat, living in lockdown conditions in barracks that were run down and infested, was not what the boys expected, and many of them quit and went back home after only two weeks. Of the 18,000 who signed up, only about 3,000 ever worked in the fields. The program ended as a spectacular failure and has mostly been forgotten.

Workplace safety was not regulated formally until 1971, when the Occupational Safety and Health Administration (OSHA) was established as the governmental body that sets safety standards for workplaces. As of 2019, OSHA has not designated a specific regulation for extreme heat, except in four jurisdictions—California, Minnesota, Washington, and the US Military (considered its own jurisdiction under OSHA). However, the Bureau of Labor Statistics reports at least 35 heat-related deaths every year. These are likely underreported, because employers themselves assign attribution. And many of these workers do not have medical insurance or paid leave, forcing them to endure inhumane conditions. When workers are paid on yield, not hourly, their days are longer, with fewer breaks, and employers rely on this.

Many of the inequalities in food production also affect those who prepare and serve our food. The concept of tipping in restaurants has been recently hotly debated, as some high-end restaurants have ended the practice at their establishments in favor of higher wages, also resulting in higher plate charges. The public reaction has been mixed, mostly because it's not yet widely adopted and tipping has always been seen as optional, a way to show gratitude for exemplary service but also a way to subjectively increase your total bill.

Following the Civil War, wealthy people in the United States who vacationed in Europe adopted the tradition of tipping, where a servant would be paid extra for going above and beyond. As the custom faded in Europe, it gained traction in the United States. When slavery ended in the United States, occupations for freed slaves were limited, and those who worked in service jobs—waiters, train porters, and the like—often were not paid wages because their employers expected their customers to leave a tip instead.

Today, tips are often pooled by the floor servers and shared on a percentage basis with others who contribute to the dining experience—hostesses, barbacks, busboys, etc. Each of these positions are legally paid well below the minimum wage ($2.13 in 18 states and Puerto Rico) because it's assumed they will make up the difference in what their employer pays them from their share of the pooled tips. California and Washington pay the highest at $11 and $12 per hour, for both tipped and nontipped positions.

Women are 71 percent of tipped servers in the United States. Waitresses are twice as likely to use Supplemental Nutrition Assistance Program (SNAP, commonly referred to as food stamps) as the rest of the population. A Cornell University study of one large national restaurant chain showed diners of all ethnicities tipped white servers higher than nonwhite servers.[57]

The $2.13 minimum wage for tip earners used to rise in tandem with the federal minimum wage, until Herman Cain, former presidential candidate and founder of the Godfather's Pizza chain, convinced a Republican held Congress to separate them. The $2.13 tipped minimum wage has not increased since 1991 (from $2.09). The US federal minimum wage was set at $7.25 in 2007 and has not increased since then. When servers don't make the difference between the tipped minimum and the nontipped minimum, their employer is supposed to make up the difference, but many don't. And the servers have limited recourse.

Most hourly workers do not have employer-provided medical insurance, paid time off, or retirement funds. Many hourly workers also stitch together several hourly jobs to earn enough to support themselves and their families, and rarely ascend beyond those low wage positions. Hours are often unpredictable and prone to last-minute changes, making childcare planning difficult if not impossible for workers with small children.

Women in tipped positions are also subjected to higher rates of sexual harassment, and because their livelihoods literally depend on their tips, they rarely can avoid the patrons behaving this way. The imbalance of power and reliance on tipped earnings creates a vulnerable place for these women. Women who work in states that have abolished the tipped minimum wage for a standard minimum for all workers report being sexually harassed at roughly half the rate of

---

[57]Lynn et al.

women in other states. Only 7 percent of the US workforce are in restaurants, but about 14 percent of all sexual harassment claims to the Equal Employment Opportunity Commission are from restaurant workers.

These injustices also apply to many of the people who work in restaurant kitchens, slaughterhouses, or work as domestic laborers. Depending on who you are and where you get your food, your plate might be completely sourced by low-wage, exploited workers. The demand for low-cost, perfectly shaped and colored, often regionally out-of-season fruits and vegetables, has created an ecosystem rife with abuse and expediency.

Up from a past that's rooted in pain I rise
—*Maya Angelou*, "Still I Rise"

Alyza Bohbot acknowledges the challenges to her woman-centric model. Her growers are smaller with lower production, and often it's difficult for her to meet demand. Their access to technology is limited by geography, aptitude, and exposure. She's forming an online marketplace to connect producers with retailers to mitigate the ebb and flow of production, but recognizes that technology is a massive inhibitor for many farmers. She also requires that workers on the farms are paid fair wages and that women do indeed have ownership in the farms, so that the revenue from City Girl Coffee goes to the women, which in turn makes stronger communities and families. The hope is that eventually, the influx of revenue will provide access to better education, technology, and tools for women, not only those in the coffee business but within these developing countries.

Janna Wagner and Jessica Sager

"Full-time mothering was a luxury
for those who could afford it."

For working parents, possibly the biggest decision they'll make during their career is whether or when to return to work after having a child. And choosing who will care for their children if they do go back to work is critical. By some estimates, childcare expenses can absorb up to 30 percent of a family's monthly income, oftentimes more than their monthly housing budget. For single earner families, the expense is often too much to manage. Without childcare, there would be many fewer women in the workplace. The burden of caregiving falls primarily on women in the United States, and the increase in dual income two-parent and single income single-parent households has not been met by an increase in childcare options.

Finding licensed, local, affordable childcare is the first step. Finding such a provider who has an opening for your child, at the time you are planning to return to work, at a rate you can afford, is frequently impossible. Finding a provider you trust, who supports your parenting approach and to whom you can pay a living wage and still manage to save enough of your paycheck to justify outsourcing your childcare is close to a miracle. All while the impossibility of finding either high-quality affordable childcare, or high-paying jobs in childcare, exists simultaneously.

When I started working full time, I had no idea how lucky I was to have the day care provider that I did. She ran a small operation from her home, and every year she would graduate one up to kindergarten and pick up a new child, usually an infant. She was an extension of our family and only called in sick once in the four years my daughter was in her care. She was loving but strict. She let me believe that all of my daughter's firsts happened on the weekends, not wanting to crush me with knowing I missed a milestone. And I only truly appreciated her reliability and consistency when my daughter went to kindergarten, when I was confronted with unpredictable snow days, random half days, and the other irregularities of a school day.

Prior to the mid '90s, low-income families that wanted one parent to stay home and care for their children were given cash assistance. When President Clinton passed the Personal Responsibility and Work Opportunity Reconciliation Act of 1996, it imposed a requirement that recipients obtain full-time work after receiving two years of benefits.

In 1999, in response to this legislation, Janna Wagner and Jessica Sager founded All Our Kin, a nonprofit based in New Haven, Connecticut, that provides comprehensive training and licensing support for people wanting to open day care facilities to solve an immediate need responding to the impact of the 1996 welfare reform.

Wagner and Sager saw an opportunity to establish a job training program for low-income women that would satisfy the work requirement of the law and create more licensed, local day care options for the communities most impacted. The All Our Kin participants were taught how to run, manage, and grow a successful small business.

Childcare has often been politicized, particularly when the notion of universal day care is discussed among legislators. It's only recently come back to the national agenda as part of Elizabeth Warren's platform in her bid for president in 2020. We almost had universal childcare in the United States in 1972, built from a similar model to our universal public schools, until a campaign claiming to protect the American Family destroyed it.

The Comprehensive Child Development Act of 1972, championed by Minnesota senator and future vice presidential candidate Walter Mondale, was vetoed by President Nixon after a propaganda campaign warning that this would outsource American families to the state. It tapped into intense fears of Communism from the Vietnam War, which was still being fought. Nixon received an unprecedented 100,000 letters opposing the bill.

Passage of the law would have provided a universal, multibillion-dollar, national day care system, allowing parents to work while leaving their young children in day care, alleviating strain on the welfare system. The bill passed the Senate 63-17 before Nixon's veto. Pat Buchanan, failed presidential nominee in the '90s, but a White House advisor at the time, helped write the veto.

In 28 states, in early 2018, a year of full-time childcare for an infant cost more than a year of fully loaded full-time public college tuition.[58] But no one is campaigning to end public college subsidies.

The Canadian Province of Quebec started a universal childcare program in 1998 under Pauline Marois, Quebec's Family Minister at the time. A family could pay $5 per day, per child, regardless of household income, for full-time childcare. Schools were also encouraged to open programs for before and after school care for students. Over 70,000 mothers were able to enter or reenter the workforce.[59]

---

[58]Digg.
[59]Hanes.

While not perfect, the program made affordable childcare options available for families and, equally as important, leveled up wages for the childcare workers it employed. The program ended in 2014 and was converted to an income-based system with public centers shifted to privately run ones.

The only fully federally funded childcare in the United States is for our military, established in 1989. And it is some of the best available. The first free public day care centers were established by the Works Progress Administration (WPA), an economic growth program started under President Franklin D. Roosevelt to provide jobs and bolster infrastructure during the Great Depression. The WPA opened close to 3,000 schools between 1933 and 1934 across 43 states. They served approximately 75,000 students.

Various private companies have worked to solve the childcare dilemma for their employees. Patagonia, the California-based, environmentally conscious outdoor outfitter, provides on-site childcare to all employees at two locations, along with paid parental leave, paid sick days, and health care. They also bus school-age children back to HQ where they can catch up with their parents before heading home as a family. They started providing onsite childcare over 30 years ago. Their CEO, Rose Marcario, is frequently asked how they can afford it, and what are the benefits—to which she clearly outlines the effect on employee engagement, loyalty, customer satisfaction, and commitment.

For the past five years, 100 percent of mothers have returned to work at Patagonia following their maternity leave. On-site childcare facilitates breastfeeding and other newborn care during the workday, easing the transition back into work, and minimizing disruption for the child.

During World War II, when much of the male workforce was temporarily replaced by women, employers seeking to hire and train women, keep productivity and profits high, and minimize workplace disruption, needed to solve their employees' childcare.

Perhaps the best example of this was the Kaiser Company (now Kaiser Permanente). Kaiser Shipyards had workers on all shifts, 364 days a year. By 1943, Kaiser employed 12,000 women in Portland, Oregon, 4,000 of whom were mothers. At the urging of Eleanor Roosevelt, Kaiser built state-of-the-art childcare facilities adjacent to their plants.

The centers were funded by US Maritime Commission. Lois Meek Stolz, noted Stanford University child psychologist and author of many books on child development, was the director of the center. They charged $5 per week for the first child and $3.75 per week for each additional child. Each day started with a physical exam to assess the health of each child. Teachers with specializations in early childhood education were recruited from all around the United States. The teachers' salaries matched those of the factory workers.

The centers were open 24 hours a day to accommodate parents on all shifts, had an infirmary, and had a fully staffed kitchen that offered prepared family meals to any worker to take home at the end of a shift.

The childcare centers were integrated and open to the children of the growing African American workforce at the shipyards; but the racial prejudice by the white families was so severe, that most black parents arranged for their own childcare. Very few African American children attended the schools.

Between November 1943 and September 1945, the Child Service Centers cared for over 4,000 young children while their parents labored in the yards.[60] They were dismantled shortly after the war, as men returned and women went back home, and have pretty much been forgotten.

---

[60]The Oregon History Project.

She wondered at the struggle Atlas had carrying

such a tiny thing on his back

—*Melissa Studdard, "Respect"*

To assist widows with young children, the state of Illinois started the Mother's Pension Act, which was then adopted by 40 states by 1920, notably before women had the right to vote, and at the same time many states were adopting workers compensation laws. The National Congress of Mothers (which later morphed into the National Parent Teacher Association) lobbied hard for the Mother's Pension Acts. The laws provided cash payments to widows and divorced or deserted women, ranging from $240 to $800 per month in today's dollars, and allowed families to remain intact. Prior to this, families suffering financial hardships often had to surrender their children to the foster care system. The only real opposition to these laws came from the charity sector, fearing displacement of their funding sources and eliminating the need for their services. The laws were also deemed as cost-saving, as foster care and adoption services incurred higher expenses than the monthly payments to the mothers.

The variations on benefits among states were due to myriad factors, mostly insofar as how eligibility was determined. Only two states—Michigan and Nebraska—included single mothers in their laws, but several others only stipulated "mothers of dependent children" without specifically mentioning marital status.

This was the beginning of publicly funded welfare. And the suspicion of the worthiness of its recipients.

The recession of the late '80s resulted in a 33 percent increase in recipients under the Aid for Families with Dependent Children (AFDC) program between 1989 and 1994. When Bill Clinton ran for President in 1992, his campaign promised "to end welfare as we have come to know it." Frances Fox Piven, famous activist and social scientist, was one of the strongest voices equating the increase in AFDC recipients with the decrease in low-wage work, which left many formerly self-sufficient workers without options. She posited in 1998 that many women on AFDC would rather work, if those jobs paid living wages and health care and childcare options were available and affordable for them.[61]

The characterization of the Welfare Queen started in the mid '70s, and was adopted and used frequently by Ronald Reagan during his (failed) 1976 and (successful) 1980 presidential campaigns. The Welfare Queen was larger than life, milking the system, and living better than you and me. She had children out of wedlock, she used fake social security cards, she drove a luxury car, and ate lobster and steak—all paid for by your tax dollars while you were hard at work, driving a late model car, eating meatloaf and mayonnaise, paying your taxes, and punching the clock. And in the mental image most people assigned to her, she was black.

Martin Gilens, a Yale University political science professor, analyzed welfare stories in print between the 1960s through 1992 and on television from 1988 through 1994. He found that in *TIME*, *Newsweek*, and *US News and World Report*, 62 percent of poverty stories featured African Americans and 65 percent of network television stories about welfare featured African Americans. More telling, perhaps, was that the magazines portrayed the lower classes as African American almost 100 percent of the time.

---

[61]Piven.

In actuality, three Welfare Queens did exist in the '70s, the most famous of whom drove her Cadillac to the Chicago public aid office before being investigated, tried, convicted, and jailed for welfare fraud in 1977. She and the two other women became representative of every woman on welfare, and those who need the benefits have lived in their shadow in the years since. When Reagan decided that their individual transgressions could represent the majority of women on welfare, when he exaggerated the benefits, luxuries, and abuses by those three women into a platform for his candidacy, he tapped into something that still resonates almost 50 years later. Even while West Virginia currently receives over 26 percent of its income from welfare programs (the national average is around 16 percent), over half of its residents are unemployed, it has the highest number of working-age people on disability, and as of the 2010 census, 93 percent of West Virginians identify as white.[62]

President Clinton passed the Temporary Assistance for Needy Families (TANF) law in 1996, capitulating to a right-leaning House, and forever changing the landscape for all of the programs lumped into the category of welfare. As best I can find, there were no women crafting this legislation, which was largely driven by Speaker Newt Gingrich. Its social goals were to encourage two-parent families, discourage births by single women, and enforce child support payments.

TANF, as it was known, imposed a number of new restrictions. Recipients were limited to five years of benefits, single teenage mothers were required to live with their parents, and recipients had to seek work or job training after two years.

It was the last piece—the work requirement—that pushed thousands of children into a childcare system that was not prepared

---

[62]CensusViewer.

to absorb them. And forced thousands of families to place their children into a system that was ripe for abuse and exploitation.

Time is a waiting woman, not some old man
with a stupid beard
—*Robin Morgan*, "Matrilineal Descent"

When two out of every three children under five years old has two parents working, and the cost of childcare for two children can be up to $18,000 a year, one parent will often take a leave from the workforce rather than put their kids into day care. And it's often a mother who is the one to stay home. Workplaces were not built to accommodate working parents. Two income households, or single-earner, single-parent households started to rise in the '70s. Childcare was often the responsibility of grandparents or relatives.

The decision to drop out of the workforce can result in lifetime financial losses of $500,000 when all of the 401(k), Social Security, and annual raises are factored for a woman in her mid-twenties who takes three years off from a $50,000 job.

Women, ironically, also face a proven wage penalty when they have children, at an average of 4 percent per child, while men average a 6 percent raise per child. The numbers are easier to determine than the cause, but the bias against working mothers is hard to refute.

Sometimes you will almost suffocate,
such joy it brings.

—*Muriel Rukeyser*, "Käthe Kollwitz"

All Our Kin currently serves four cities in Connecticut, and has recently opened in the Bronx in New York City. Their five-year plan includes extending into other major metropolitan areas while not growing so quickly as to compromise the quality of their service. Their clients come through referrals from others who have gone through the program, many of whom are already providing care to their families and friends, but aren't licensed or haven't been trained. All Our Kin covers the entire range of skills for a childcare provider, from legal, financial, medical, and early education. The providers form tight networks in their communities and learn from and share with each other, elevating the experience for themselves, the parents, and most importantly, the children.

Janna Wagner talks about watching their clients move from seeing themselves as babysitters to teachers, becoming successful business owners, and mentors to other new clients in the program.

A client who lived in government-subsidized housing for low-income people came to All Our Kin and got her day care license about 10 years ago. She and her husband continued working with All Our Kin to get coaching and stay current on creative ideas and approaches, while working in janitorial services at hospitals for additional income. Eventually, their daughter started working with them and then the husband got his own license and started a separate program. Their day care grew so fast they had a waitlist, they were able to buy a multifamily home in a mixed-income neighborhood, and they are now one of the most in-demand centers with offerings for both infants and preschoolers.

A 2015 assessment compared All Our Kin providers with a group not associated with All Our Kin to assess the efficacy of the All Our Kin program.[63] Results showed that All Our Kin providers scored significantly higher on nationally accredited measurements of quality in childcare, and more than half of current All Our Kin providers planned to stay in the childcare field, compared to only seven percent of the non-All Our Kin affiliated group.

In general, it's much harder for parents of children with disabilities to find day care to accommodate their specific needs. Family childcare providers are much more likely to take in those children and individualize their care. In Connecticut, there is a state program called Help Me Grow that assists parents in early detection of various disabilities, and each All Our Kin provider is trained in how to do this and work with the parents to obtain the right intervention and assistance. All Our Kin also works with providers to teach medication administration as another differentiator to serve their communities.

Between 2000 and 2011, Connecticut lost nearly 34 percent of its family childcare programs—leaving 8,100 fewer childcare spaces for Connecticut's families. All Our Kin has increased, by 74 percent, the number of licensed family childcare programs in New Haven during the same period.[64] The University of Connecticut's Center for Economic Analysis finds that each provider licensed by All Our Kin enables between four and five parents to enter the workforce.

---

[63]Nelson.
[64]All Our Kin.

Solving the childcare problem in the way that Janna Wagner and Jessica Sager have, by bringing more providers into the business of childcare and bringing more licensed centers into neighborhoods with families that need skilled childcare, puts more women in the workforce, providing fair wages and skilled work, encourages more small business growth, and reinvestment in community.

Amy Pence-Brown

"Why am I fat and happy?"

At what point in your life did you start to love yourself? And I don't mean liking yourself, being pleased by your looks, being proud of your accomplishments. I mean really truly loving yourself with the fullness of your whole self. Without requiring any external validation. Just you.

Many of us never get there. But damn, is it obvious when you see it shine from within another woman.

I sometimes still hear the criticisms of former friends and boyfriends, ones whose calls I'd send into voicemail now, but their comments on my looks, my ambitions, my failings are as loud as the day they said them. Do I remember the compliments, the unsolicited ones, and hear them as loudly as many years later and at those critical times when I need a boost? I don't. And most of us don't either.

Each of the chapters you've read so far in this book are stories of incredible women. Women who have overcome massive systemic barriers to success. Women who are using their power to open that path for others, so that they can achieve the same—or more—success without having to fight as hard.

But I'm guessing each of them also had moments, months, perhaps years, of crushing self-doubt, self-loathing, and impostor syndrome. And maybe they still have flashes of those emotions on occasion.

Amy Pence-Brown's story is included here, specifically last, because I hope that your inspiration reading each of the stories in the previous chapters will remove some of your self-imposed barriers to success and show you how you can also create a bigger space for others in your workplace, your community, and your life.

The hot coals of four centuries of white male approval

—*Audre Lorde*, "Power"

Amy Pence-Brown became famous for standing for an hour in a bikini in the middle of a farmer's market in Boise, Idaho, in August of 2015. A fat, 40-year-old mother of three. Blindfolded. Baring cellulite and stretch marks. But she stood in front of a sign that asked, "I'm standing for anyone who has struggled with a self-esteem issue like me. If you believe all bodies are valuable draw a heart on my body." They did. They also embraced her, and cried with her, and whispered to her. In Pence-Brown, some likely saw their own imperfect bodies, with stretch marks and cellulite. But they also saw courage, vulnerability, and self-love. And maybe even a mirror of themselves. When she took off the blindfold, Pence-Brown was covered in dozens of hearts, in words of love, support, and gratitude.

The video went viral, and her moment caught the attention of people all over the world.[65]

The first time I watched it, I gasped. To do what she did, and the way she did it, was remarkable. Then I cried. I was so moved by the reactions of the strangers around her. Then I got fired up about telling her story and sharing the power of it with as many people as I can.

We're taught from our first years how our society values women. We're bombarded with advertising images promoting perfect skin, perfect hair, perfect bodies. It's only very recently that advertisers have widened their lens on defining beauty and welcomed diverse models.

How does self-doubt become so deeply lodged in our psyches? How is that voice, the one that tells us we're unworthy, inadequate, undesirable, becomes the one we hear above all the others?

Many of us grew up playing with Barbie, not really thinking about her forced tip-toes, erased genitalia, or lack of career options in the '70s and '80s. In 2011, a Hamilton College student[66] who had battled eating disorders decided to extrapolate Barbie into a full-size woman. She stood six feet tall, had a 39-inch bust, an 18-inch waist, and a size three shoe. The average American woman is five feet, four inches tall, with a 38-inch bust, a 37-inch waist, and a size 8.5 shoe. And she has genitals and feet that flex.

Unrealistic expectations on standards for beauty are written early.

My childhood was full of boys and sports, and probably set me back a bit when it came to caring about my appearance. I didn't have an older sister or anyone to guide me through things like eyeliner, shaving, or other fundamental female rituals. And honestly, I still struggle with them. I was an unusually skinny kid, and somehow

---

[65]TEDx Talks, "Amy Pence-Brown."
[66]Slayen.

it was acceptable to remark on that, in very different ways than the way people talked to and about the fat kids. When I started school, it was a traditional Catholic school with uniforms that tried to equalize us all, regardless of socioeconomic status or body shape. The things about which I became self-conscious were my frizzy, curly hair—which could not, no matter what I tried, be convinced to feather, which was The Way To Wear Your Hair in the late '70s and early '80s—and my translucently white skin, which would burn and blister every summer. It wasn't until I was pregnant that I developed breasts, which was just fine as I didn't want to bother with bras or anything fancy anyway.

---

the wrong skin the wrong nose the wrong hair the
wrong need the wrong dream
—*June Jordan*, "A Poem About My Rights"

The rise of Instagram certainly hasn't helped bolster the self-esteem of our young women and men. Manufactured perfectionism, created with filters and fake backgrounds, heightens the insecurities of preteens in particular.

In 2017, 55 percent of plastic surgeons reported an increase in patients wanting to improve their appearance in selfies, up 13 percent in just one year.[67] In 2013, thigh gap—the space between

---

[67]McCall.

your thighs when standing erect—became a thing, followed soon after by bikini bridge, which is when (while you are lying down) your bikini bottom lies across your hip bones without touching your stomach. Blogs, videos, hashtags, books, and workouts were launched to help people achieve something impossible for most of us, unhealthy for many of us, and unknown by all of us prior to its moment of fame. It got so bad that Pinterest, the popular site for collecting and cataloging images from the web, started serving up PSAs for eating disorder services when users would search for images of thigh gap.

How insidious is this ideal of perfection, that it seeps into how we judge ourselves against others, how we react to those around us, how we talk to ourselves when our children are listening and internalizing what we value? And how do we undo that damage?

After years of being served perfection from the media, from social channels, from our dolls, and our own ideals, seeing authentic bodies and women can be jarring. Seeing more bodies that more closely resemble our own in those places is still unusual, but advertisers and others are starting to get it.

In 2016, *Sports Illustrated* featured Ashley Graham—a proud plus-size model—on their annual swimsuit issue cover (although I need to mention, the year before, they featured Robyn Lawley, who is a size 12, and the fans called her plus-size). The magazine started the swimsuit edition in 1964, mostly to maintain readership and attention between the Superbowl and baseball season, but it is widely credited for launching the era of the supermodel. It wasn't until 1997 that they featured a black woman—Tyra Banks—on the cover. That was the same year they featured the first nonmodel, Steffi Graf, a professional tennis player and only winner of the Golden Slam (all four Grand Slam titles and an Olympic gold medal in the same year), which she won in 1988, and for which she appeared on the cover of a regular, non-swimsuit edition *Sports Illustrated*.

Israel, Italy, Spain, and France all have legislation banning underweight models, a response to the spike in anorexia, mostly (over 90 percent) affecting women. Digitally altered images must also self-report as such, after many were found to show women thinner than the standard for anorexia diagnosis. Repeated exposure to hyper-thinness conditions us into thinking that it is normal, which directly influences positive and healthy body image.

Of the 300 fashion brands at the 2018 New York Fashion Week, only 32 produce clothing in sizes up to 16.

Body dissatisfaction is a leading indicator across the spectrum of women's health, affecting self-esteem, eating patterns and disorders, social anxiety, and depression. Overweight women are so often dismissed or shamed by medical professionals, that they delay or avoid altogether regular doctor visits and preventative care.

Our obsession with unrealistic ideals of fitness and beauty is deeply embedded in our self-image, and our perception of suitable partners and social circles. These biases are built from our youngest ages, reinforced over years of imagery and advertisements, and take root in how we raise our children to perceive themselves, often unconsciously. As parents, we monitor our children's diets, but they also overhear and internalize our own insecurities about our bodies. When we remark to each other how good someone looks, and what about them we admire, our children—and particularly our daughters—hear that and use that as the place from which they measure their worth.

Thinness as a beauty ideal is big business.

The weight loss market in the United States is valued at $66 billion per year. Close to 70 percent of all American women are plus size (size 14 and higher). About 71 percent of Americans are overweight, and have the highest rate of obesity in the world, at 66 percent of adults, and 17 percent of children, when obesity is defined as having a body mass index higher than 30 percent.

Approximately 70 million adults in United States are obese (evenly split by gender) while 99 million are overweight (45 million men and 54 million women).[68] Obesity, for the first time in 2017, was cited as the cause for more preventable early deaths than smoking.

The United States ranks highest for average daily sugar consumption, which is not surprising when considering how many packaged and processed foods and drinks contain added sugars, mainly in the form of high fructose corn syrup. By the time a child in the United States is three or four, they know not only the McDonalds logo, but what they want to order before they've even arrived at the restaurant. Our reliance on convenience foods, which are often cheaper than healthier alternatives, perpetuates a cycle of unhealthy eating, precarious medical conditions, and chronic illness.

We simultaneously market physical perfection and sugar consumption to our kids, and wonder why they're sick and unhappy.

By far the most well known, and most popular weight loss program in the United States is Weight Watchers, which was founded in the 1960s by Jan Nidetch, who went public in 1968 and became wealthy almost overnight with her community-based system. In 2016 it reported $1.2 billion in revenues and 3.5 million active members, the majority of whom are women (Weight Watchers did not respond to my requests for member profile data). In 2018, it offered free memberships to teenagers, aiming to teach them life-long good eating habits and choices. In 2019, it announced new branding—WW (Weight Watchers Reimagined)—and a shift from only weight and diet goals to fitness and general health and wellness.

But 80 percent of people who lose weight eventually gain all or most of it back, creating an unhealthy and untenable cycle toward

---

[68]U.S. Department of Health and Human Services.

increased dissatisfaction with ourselves for failing at something, and not reaching that perfect body type.

If you've not yet tuned into the magic that is Lizzo, you're missing out. The multifaceted, African American, plus-size entertainer is just hitting mainstream recognition, thanks in part to her feature in *Playboy's* Spring 2019 issue. Since the magazine's founding in 1953, she is the second full-figure woman ever in the magazine. (The first was a white woman, Molly Constable, in 2017). Lizzo brings a beautiful energy to her performances, loves herself and her outsized personality, makes no apologies for any of it, and isn't afraid to incorporate her mad flute skills into her act.

Shrill, a delightful sitcom from Hulu, centers on Annie, played masterfully by Aidy Bryant from *Saturday Night Live*. It is based on the 2016 autobiography of Lindy West, a journalist and body positivity activist. Its first season has gotten strong critical praise for the portrayal of a woman with a full life and successful career, who happens to be fat. She is smart, strong, well dressed, confident, and most notably for a character of her size, not dieting. The show delves into her work life, her personal relationships, and her self-esteem without making her the butt of jokes, or a pariah.

We witness her romantic relationship and cheer for her to dump the man child, even as he goes from the guy who makes her leave through the back door to the guy who shows up to care for her dog in a pinch. We sit in her apartment with her equally lovable roommate and want to drink wine and gossip with them. We think the trainer who stalks her and tries to encourage her is a total bitch. It's a revolutionary show, by making the main character someone we feel we know, that we really like, that we don't mock or pity, and that we genuinely care about.

There is a scene where Annie goes to a pool party exclusively for fat women, and it's one of the most joyful scenes I've ever seen with women in bathing suits, regardless of their size. There's a vibe of pure pleasure among these women.

This Is Us, a hit series from NBC, features Kate, one of the three central characters, who is morbidly obese. Her weight is a strong thread throughout the storylines, starting when she meets her future husband at a weight loss support group, to jeopardizing her chances of becoming pregnant. Her weight is a major theme of many of the flashbacks to her younger years. She's written as more sympathetic than Annie in *Shrill*, but we are participating in her journey and cheering for her also, but from a different perspective.

By casting these women in two major roles, both of which are receiving lots of positive reviews from fans, and supported by strong writing and casts, these networks are challenging stereotypes and assumptions. I hope this trend continues with more complex, fully formed characters across a number of genres and platforms.

She gorged on bitterness without a name
—*Christina Rossetti*, "Goblin Market"

A my Pence-Brown is hoping to fix the perception of fat women by fixing our mindset around weight and self-acceptance. She runs RADCAMP: A Body Positive Boot Camp for Feminist Teens, a weekend for teens (and a separate one for women) to reinforce body positivity at a time when our ideas of our self-worth are formed and fixed. That voice you sometimes still hear, the one telling you that you're too something or not enough something? That's your teenaged insecure self still criticizing you for just being you. Pence-Brown hopes that by bringing girls together for a few days in a safe, nonjudgmental place, they can lift each other while exploring what it means to be beautiful, strong, female, loved, and valued.

Because loving and accepting yourself also allows you to more fully love and accept those around you. And from there, generosity flows.

In Closing

The world is changing. I have to believe this. The publication date of this book changed several times because of the rate at which the issues I've discussed are changing.

The common themes among each of the stories are undeniable. Access to power. Equal protection under the law. Shifting the focus away from our physical worth to our intellectual worth. Access to money, property, and education. Building or breaking systems to make them work for all of us. Getting a chance to show our capabilities, our value, our intelligence. The ways in which women seek not only to enrich themselves but to extend that to other women, some they may never know.

Power structures are shifting. Women hold more seats in Congress than ever before, women are ascending into positions of power and influence in corporations in record numbers, women are changing the game, finally; not just the rules by which the games are played.

More men are stepping up to be vocal allies, and working on behalf of those of us who do this work every day. And as long as there will be men who only listen to other men, we need more of you to be advocating with us.

I hope you've learned something new while reading this book. New names, new perspectives, new elements to stories you thought you knew. I hope you share these stories and add them to your "hey did you know" collection of cocktail party stories. I hope you raise your children and grandchildren with a wider understanding of what women have done, and what women can do.

There is still so much to do. My daughter's career is already in full throttle, so while it's hardly too late for her, I'm much more optimistic for those still in diapers. It's on all of us to work toward a better, safer, healthier, freer, more equal world for us all.

We need to advocate strongly for women in positions of power. Not every woman, but all women. What I mean by that is, give women your support at the same level you give it to men with the same ambitions. Give it more, because she probably needs it more. Let the world hear and see you standing with her. Let her be imperfect, let her make mistakes. We deserve that. We have earned that.

Open the world for your daughters. Travel with them, introduce them to everything that sparks their interest. Girl Scouts is a great gateway for girls toward self-reliance and confidence, in a welcoming, supportive environment. Challenge yourself to break away from your comfort zone if that's what it takes. Grow with her. Show her through your strength and example that fear is something to be faced, not something to which we should give any power. Steer her perceptions of beauty toward her personality, not her body.

Challenge your sons, and your son's friends, and their parents, to be and to raise and to extol them to be the men we need. Let them explore their femininity, let them cry, let them hug. Make sexism as uncool as racism or homophobia. Don't force them into rigid definitions of masculinity.

Raise more James Shaws, fewer Brock Turners.

Broaden your definition of success to include those with paths that are not linear. Take into account the tenacity and courage required to stay on that path, rather than one that had been groomed for them.

In June of 2016, I was honored to be invited by the Obama White House to attend The United State of Women Summit, among 5,000 others who advocate daily for women and girls. President Obama's words that day moved me deeply, and I feel it is a fitting way to close this book, because I still believe we can have a feminist president, and elect leaders who stand for equality regardless of gender, ability, race, sexual orientation, or citizenship.

We admire the men who shaped our country, and rightfully so, the men we see as heroes—from Alexander Hamilton to Muhammad Ali—for their confidence and their courage in believing they could change our nation, this idea of self-creation, that there's nothing holding us back. In them, we see America itself, constantly reinventing itself, fearless, looking out over the horizon at the next frontier.

But our country is not just all about the Benjamins— it's about the Tubmans, too. We need all our young people to know that Clara Barton and Lucretia Mott and Sojourner Truth and Eleanor Roosevelt and Dorothy Height, those aren't just for Women's History Month. They're the authors of our history, women who shaped their destiny. They need to know that.

A woman did not magically appear on a space shuttle. It took Sally Ride's relentless commitment, Mae Jemison's boundless courage to shatter that glass ceiling. A group of California farmworkers—they weren't just handed their rights. It took Dolores Huerta organizing and mobilizing, fighting for the dignity and justice they deserved.

Rosa Parks wasn't simply a tired seamstress who sat down by accident. She was a civil rights leader with the eye of a strategist and the heart of a warrior. She had the confidence to board on that bus, the courage to risk her own life and liberty for the sake of ours. History did not fall into her lap—she seized that moral arc and she bent it with her bare hands in the direction of justice.

That's the story that's still being written, today, by our modern-day heroes like Nancy Pelosi or Sonia Sotomayor or Billie Jean King or Laverne Cox or Sheryl Sandberg or Oprah Winfrey or Mikaila Ulmer or Michelle Obama—the countless ordinary people every day who are bringing us closer to our highest ideals. That's the story we're going to keep on telling, so our girls see that they, too, are America—confident and courageous and, in the words of Audre Lorde, "deliberate and afraid of nothing."

That's the country we love, and I've never been optimistic—as optimistic as I am now that we're going to create a country where everybody, no matter who they are or what they look like or where they come from or who they love, can make of their lives what they will. And together, we can build a world that's more just and more prosperous and more free. That's a job for all of us.
—*President Barack Obama*, June 16, 2016[69].

---

[69]Obama.

Many of us are still building that world, but we need more of us, and more of you, to be vocal advocates for the world in which we wish to live. Find the place where you can be an advocate and commit to it. There's room for everyone, I promise.

Don't put this book on your shelf. Share it, reference it, remind yourself of the tasks and tactics throughout and try to employ a new one in your workplace, and in your life, every day, every week, every month.

Building a World for Everyone

In my work, people frequently ask me, how they can be a better ally, especially if they are not a woman? The list below is intended to be a launch point for those of you who have read this far and are earnestly seeking ways to improve the world around you for everyone. And the suggestions are in no way limited to how you work with women; they should apply to all of your interactions. I welcome your additions to this list, as well as your thoughts on their efficacy.

Open more doors into more powerful rooms.
Find opportunities at your organizations to bring talented women into the rooms with the big tables where the big decisions are made.

Require your talent pipeline to be diverse.
Seek to fill your organization with the best and brightest, without regard to their demographics. Evaluate how well your employee referral program is toward achieving this. (Most are best at bringing in more of the same.)

Offer promotions and assignments to those you think "can't" because of family obligations.
Don't create a narrative for your workforce based on your own preferences and assumptions. Evaluate their performance without considering their constraints as you perceive them.

Model the Salesforce "Women's Surge" for meetings and events.
Salesforce requires that at least 30 percent of all attendees in meetings and speakers at events are women. I'd challenge you to go beyond and also mandate inclusion of people of color. And strive for 50 percent.

Share stories.
Aubrey Blanche, Global Head of Diversity and Inclusion at Atlassian, says, "asking for a narrative instead of criticism can diffuse tension, prevent disagreement, and promote mutual understanding." Build trust and pull toward the center.

Fund the affinity groups.
Offer bonuses to the leaders who step up to run the various affinity programs in your organization. Allow budget for programming, speakers, offsite events, and incentives.

Tap the unofficial leaders.
Every organization has them. The people who don't want to be line managers, but who the rest of the team turns to for insight, guidance, mentorship, advice. Utilize them informally to create change.

Call out obnoxious behavior.
Not just the blatant harassment. The small, seemingly innocuous comments about a coworker's sexuality, shape, partner, fuckability,

whatever. Do not tolerate it, do not laugh at it, do not encourage it. The more allies who do this, the better the workplace will become for all of us.

Listen. And believe.
When women say they've been harassed or assaulted, listen to them. Believe them.

Defend.
When others talk about harassment, stand up for the victim. Assume they are telling the truth, and encourage those around you to do the same. Office gossip is vicious and damning.

Focus on the work.
You don't have to like working with everyone. None of us are capable of that. But when you speak of coworkers, focus on the quality of their work. Don't make it personal.

Be on high alert at events.
Mixing clients, conferences, and booze, frequently brings out some pretty awful behavior. Instead of being the one consuming all the cocktails, be aware of situations your coworkers may find themselves in and unable to easily escape. Your interruption and redirect can be incredibly helpful.

Teach good sex (and consent).
Don't shy away from teaching your kids about the biology of sex. Talk with your partner(s) about their bodies, encourage them to know their boundaries and their preferences, and how and when to say yes or no. Good, healthy, satisfying sex starts with good, healthy communication.

Strive for a safe place.

I've worked with colleagues going through divorce, death, coming out, and other massive life events. By not encouraging gossip, by fostering a workplace that supports everyone regardless of life stage, you will engender stronger loyalty and happier colleagues.

Quit assigning narratives.

Take people at face value. Don't assume you know where they're at just because you might have known someone in their situation, or you maybe once breezed by a similar place. Let them tell you who they are, and what they can do.

Hire on value, not previous salary history.

It's now illegal in some states to ask an applicant's previous salary history, but even if it's still legal where you are, establish the budget for the position and hire based on the applicant's value to your organization relative to the assigned budget.

Consider factors outside of work when an employee's patterns change.

When a punctual employee is frequently late, consider what might have changed at home. Provide a way for that employee to share confidentially the challenge they're having without fear of being judged, gossiped about, or fired.

Stop working outside of work.

Please. If there is one thing we can all do to bless each other in the 21st century, it's this. If you're a team leader, don't send emails after 7 p.m. or before 7 a.m. And never on weekends, unless it's truly critical. If you're afraid you'll lose the thought, save it as a draft and send it Monday morning. Protect the private lives of your employees. Allow them to step off.

Know your legislators.

Make sure the people writing the laws for your town, your state, your country are considering the consequences for all of us when they do. Get involved, know the positions of each candidate and each incumbent, and support those who support the widest representation of their electorate.

Review your employee referral program.

I realize it saves you time and money but is it really creating the workforce you want? Or is it just bringing in people who look and behave like your current employees? If you want to build a diverse workforce, you need to evaluate how you build your talent pipeline.

Reimburse for childcare when you host after hours events.

Not everyone can attend the after work happy hour, the client dinner, the team bonding exercise outside of work hours. Offer to reimburse your team for childcare so they can attend.

Require lactation rooms at all office locations and at event sites.

This likely only affects a small percentage of your workers or event attendees, but not only is it greatly appreciated, it also makes a powerful statement about your values as an organization.

Examine your own biases.

Not publicly. No one wants to see that. But honestly peel back your deeply rooted biases against certain people. Seek to understand from where they come, and if the recipient has truly earned your negative response. Most often, they haven't.

Acknowledge that your silence perpetuates inequality.

Saying nothing isn't being safe or politically correct, it implies consent or support. When you say nothing, whatever bad behavior is on display gets a pass, and will continue. Change comes when people speak up and out. Be that kind of advocate.

Provide free feminine hygiene products.
Add it to your office operating budget. Imagine having to plan for, carry, pay tax on, and remember toilet paper every time you paid a visit? Accommodate all of your employees. Menstruating is miserable enough, making it less so is just the right thing to do.

Attend and participate in Workplace Affinity Programs.
If your employer hosts events or programs for Women, LGBTQ, minorities, or ethnicities, participate in them and bring your teammates. The more people contributing to these conversations from a place of learning, the stronger the team becomes.

Create opportunities.
When you have a key client meeting, invite the person who is critical to the project but who never gets invited to the meeting. Bring them in. Coach them beforehand, give them ownership of part of the agenda, let them shine. You don't need to control everything.

Criticize equally.
Be just as critical of a woman's performance as you would a man's. Ignore gender when assessing an employee. Be factual, specific, and honest.

Wield your power.
Al Davis, legendary coach and owner of the Oakland Raiders, twice refused to allow the team to play in segregated cities. Marc Benioff, CEO of Salesforce, threatened to close their Indiana offices when in 2015 Governor Mike Pence signed a law allowing businesses to refuse customers based on religious beliefs. Pence changed the law.

Abandon the meritocracy.
The model is broken. Burn down your evaluation criteria and processes and start anew. Not everyone succeeds across the same set of metrics, but everyone can be successful. Discover deeper ways of evaluating and rewarding your employees.

Be generous.
One of the best managers I ever had deflected every team achievement back to the team. He would follow the company-wide emails with a note to our team, our VPs, and his leadership outlining the contributions of each person on the team. It bred loyalty, cohesion, success, and pride. Do it.

Breed a culture of candor.
Allow your teams to share their ideas on what's broken, and how to best fix it. Ennoble them to own the solutions. Assign a budget every year toward these initiatives. Reward those who step up, even if they fail.

Advocate for benefits that don't directly benefit you.
Everyone wins when every employee feels valued and appreciated. Even if you don't need to take paid family leave, encourage your employer to offer it if it benefits others around you.

Let people enjoy their time off.
This goes with not sending emails on the weekends. But seriously, I worked at a firm that congratulated women who made quota while on maternity leave. Don't be that company. Let your employees enjoy their newborns, their well-earned rest. And if they do make quota? Be cognizant of the message you send to other women in the way you speak of it.

Hear the mansplaining and the manterrupting.
Don't ignore when a man runs over the end of a woman's sentence, or finishes it for her. If she doesn't, stop him and ask her to finish. Look him in the eye and control the room. He probably doesn't realize he's doing it, but he will after that.

Move from mentoring to sponsoring.
Learnings tend to go in one direction when mentoring. Be a sponsor. Take in as much as you send out. Sponsoring requires advocacy and identifying opportunities. Discover and share.

Canvass regularly your employees.
Take the temperature of your organization. Don't assume you know. Corporate dynamics change frequently and imperceptibly overnight. Be open to feedback, and committed to evolution.

Make meetings and events accessible to all.
According to Sheri Byrne-Haber, a Certified Professional in Accessibility Core Competencies (CPACC), meeting and event planners can do much better planning around accessibility. She encourages everyone to consider the safety of all attendees. Is there an accessible entry and exit for everyone? Are there captions for video presentations, and interpreters for speakers? Broaden your idea of the experience for every attendee and commit to being wholly inclusive.

End your unpaid internship program.
Keep hiring the interns, but pay them. Unpaid internships exclude a lot of talent that cannot afford not to be paid during summers. Pay them fairly for the work they perform.

Creatively uncover potential and promise.
Reach beyond your core pipeline and identify potential. Invest in problem solvers. Seek criticism from successful people. None of it is personal, and it will make you better.

Check in with the front lines.
No matter your role in the company, know what happens on the front lines with your customers. Know how those employees are doing. What brings them satisfaction and breeds loyalty. This is essential to your success, and so many executives miss it.

Speak of the WE.
Another attribute of strong, generous leaders is they never speak of ME. They talk about WE, the team, the achievement of the group as a whole. It is never about them, individually.

Ignore the Human Resources department.
I don't really mean that. But do not rely on your HR department to be the voice of your employees. They are not. Realize that if you are an executive, chances are your HR department isn't passing on bad news to you. In all seriousness, HR protects you. Employees are never honest with HR. Get in the trenches and listen to your teams.

Accept that not everyone wants the same things.
Some of your coworkers are perfectly happy where they are. Climbing the ladder isn't a goal for everyone. It doesn't make them less ambitious, less committed, less anything. It probably makes them great at their current job, and an excellent source for ideas on how to improve it.

Be Stuart and Laura.
You don't have to be the lone member of the First Club. Find and foster that alliance. Make each other better, stronger, smarter. Build a friendship that will grow and broker other good things in each direction. Challenge each other to keep that bar high.

Be Cindy.
Sit in the places that make other people squirm. Question assumptions and conventions. Ask people to question theirs. And have great (or better) sex!

Be Janna and Jessica.
Find people who complement your skill set and share your passion. Team with them to make change. Create new models that solve problems up and down stream.

Be Kerry.
Find a way to speak with strength on behalf of others who will never be around the tables you inhabit. Be their advocate, their sponsor, their voice.

Be Maria and Stacy.
Get in the fight when you see or experience injustice. Rally your advocates and make enough noise to spark positive institutional change. Raise your voice for those who can't or won't.

Be Connie and Woody.
Make mentorship a core value in your interactions with every coworker. Look for unique talents and find ways to capitalize on them, both for the employee benefit and for your organization. Don't rely on traditional career paths, or assume that people know where they can truly excel.

Be Alyza.

Consider ways in which a tweak, or an overhaul, to your business model can lift others. It may be your suppliers, it may be your customers, it may be both. Allow yourself to step back and reevaluate at least once a year.

Be Arlan and Susan.

Take risks on promising ideas for which the greater market may not be ready. Smart people will succeed, and your investment in them will pay off. Recreate your own model for what wins.

Be your own Amy.

Allow yourself to truly love yourself. Train your mind to quiet the negativity from within. Hear the kind and sincere things other people say about you. Be generous with your praise and perception of what's beautiful about others, and yourself.

This section can be downloaded via inthecompanyofmenbook.com.
If you'd like to license it or distribute more than 10 copies, please contact me via inthecompanyofmenbook.com/contact.

Resources

Adams, Abigail. "Letter from Abigail Adams to John Adams, 31 March–5 April 1776." Massachusetts Historical Society. http://www.masshist.org/digitaladams/archive/doc?id=L1776 0331aa&bc=%2Fdigitaladams%2Farchive%2Fbrowse%2Flett ers_1774_1777.php

All Our Kin. "Our Impact." http://www.allourkin.org/our-impact

American College of Pediatricians. "The Impact of Pornography on Children." June 2016. https://www.acpeds.org/the-college-speaks/position-statements/the-impact-of-pornography-on-children

Babson College. "Women Entrepreneurs 2014: Bridging the Gender Gap in Venture Capital." The Diana Project. September 2014. http://www.babson.edu/Academics/centers/blank-center/global-research/diana/Documents/diana-project-executive-summary-2014.pdf

Brush, Candida. "Women Entrepreneurs: Bridging The Gender Gap In Venture Capital." Forbes. September 30, 2014. https://www.forbes.com/sites/babson/2014/09/30/women-entrepreneurs-bridging-the-gender-gap-in-venture-capital/#4ee63bfc3360

Brush, Candida, Patricia Greene, Lakshmi Balachandra, and Amy Davis. "The gender gap in venture capital—progress, problems, and perspectives." *Venture Capital: An International Journal of Entrepreneurial Finance*. 20, no. 2 (2018): 115-136. https://www.tandfonline.com/doi/full/10.1080/13691066.2017.1349266?scroll=top&needAccess=true

Buckley, Cara. "A.C.L.U., Citing Bias Against Women, Wants Inquiry Into Hollywood's Hiring Practices." *New York Times*. May 12, 2015. https://www.nytimes.com/2015/05/13/movies/aclu-citing-bias-against-women-wants-inquiry-into-hollywoods-hiring-practices.html

Bureau of Labor Statistics. "Labor Force Statistics from the Current Population Survey." https://www.bls.gov/cps/documentation.htm#comp

Burhouse, Susan, Karyen Chu, Keith Ernst, Ryan Goodstein, Alicia Lloro, Gregory Lyons, Joyce Northwood, Yazmin Osaki, Sherrie Rhine, Dhruv Sharma, and Jeffrey Weinstein. "FDIC National Survey of Unbanked and Underbanked Households." October 20, 2016. https://www.economicinclusion.gov/surveys/2015household/documents/2015_FDIC_Unbanked_Underbanked_HH_Survey_ExecSumm.pdf

Caggiano, Reverend Frank. "Bishop's Letter Announcing New Leadership Model At St. Anthony." Diocese of Bridgeport, Connecticut. December 9, 2018. https://www.bridgeportdiocese.org/bishop-announces-new-leadership-model/

CensusViewer. "Population of West Virginia: Census 2010 and 2000 Interactive Map, Demographics, Statistics, Quick Facts." http://censusviewer.com/state/WV

Chandelier Creative. "Watch Our First Documentary: 'Join the Social Sex Revolution.'" February 9, 2017. https://www.chandeliercreative.com/article/watch-our-first-documentary-join-the-social-sex-revolution

Clance, Pauline Rose and Suzanne Imes. "The Imposter Phenomenon in High Achieving Women: Dynamics and Therapeutic Intervention." *Psychotherapy Theory, Research and Practice.* 15, no. 3 (Fall 1978). http://www.paulineroseclance.com/pdf/ip_high_achieving_women.pdf

Clark, Kate. "Mary Meeker raises $1.25B for Bond, her debut growth fund." TechCrunch. April 24, 2019. https://techcrunch.com/2019/04/24/mary-meeker-raises-1-25b-for-bond-her-debut-growth-fund/

Dargis, Manohla. "Sundance Fights Tide With Films Like 'The Birth of a Nation.'" *New York Times.* January 29, 2016. https://www.nytimes.com/2016/01/30/movies/sundance-fights-tide-with-films-like-the-birth-of-a-nation.html

Digg. "The Cost Of Childcare Vs. College Tuition In All 50 States, Visualized." November 28, 2018. http://digg.com/2018/childcare-vs-college-tuition-by-state

Evans, Will and Sinduja Rangarajan. "Hidden figures: How Silicon Valley keeps diversity data secret." Reveal from The Center for Investigative Reporting. October 19, 2017. https://www.revealnews.org/article/hidden-figures-how-silicon-valley-keeps-diversity-data-secret/

FindLaw. "Sex Education in Public Schools." http://education.findlaw.com/curriculum-standards-school-funding/sex-education-in-public-schools.html

Fleximize. "Ventures of the PayPal Mafia." https://fleximize.com/paypal-mafia/

Freeman, Mike. "The Past, Present and Future of Women and the NFL's 'Boys Club.'" Bleacher Report. March 21, 2016. https://bleacherreport.com/articles/2618710-the-past-present-and-future-of-women-and-

Fugler, JP. "Why the Lack of Women in Educational Leadership Matters." HuffPost. Updated Jul 01, 2016. https://www.huffpost.com/entry/lack-of-women-in-education_b_7708220

Glass, Jeremy. "8 Ways Porn Influenced Technology." Thrillist. February 14, 2014. https://www.thrillist.com/vice/how-porn-influenced-technology-8-ways-porn-influenced-tech-supercompressor-com

Green, Jeff, Hannah Recht, and Mathieu Benhamou. "Wanted: 3,732 Women to Govern Corporate America." Bloomberg Business Week. March 21, 2019. https://www.bloomberg.com/graphics/2019-women-on-boards/

Gregory, Mollie. *Women Who Run the Show: How a Brilliant and Creative New Generation of Women Stormed Hollywood.* New York: Macmillan, 2003.

Guttmacher Institute. "American Adolescents' Sources of Sexual Health Information." December 2017. https://www.guttmacher.org/fact-sheet/facts-american-teens-sources-information-about-sex#

Hamilton, Arlan. "Dear White Venture Capitalists: If you're reading this, it's (almost!) too late." Medium. June 13, 2015. https://medium.com/female-founders/dear-white-venture-capitalists-if-you-re-not-actively-searching-for-and-seeding-qualified-4f382f6fd4a7

Hanes, Allison. "The policies and politics of early childhood education." *Montreal Gazette.* May 4, 2017. http://montrealgazette.com/opinion/columnists/allison-hanes-the-policies-and-politics-of-early-childhood-education

Humphreys, Jeffrey. "The Multicultural Economy 2013." The University of Georgia Terry College of Business. 2013. http://latinodonorcollaborative.org/wp-content/uploads/2015/12/Multicultural-Economy-2013-SELIG-Center.pdf

Ickeringill, Nan. "For Luncheon Clubs, Food is of Secondary Importance." *New York Times.* April 23,1967. https://www.nytimes.com/1967/04/23/archives/for-luncheon-clubs-food-is-of-secondary-importance.html

International Trade Forum. "Women in Coffee." *International Trade Forum Magazine*. 3 (April 2008). http://www.tradeforum.org/Women-in-Coffee/

Jungnickel, Katrina. "'One needs to be very brave to stand all that': Cycling, rational dress and the struggle for citizenship in late nineteenth century Britain." *Geoforum*. 64 (August 2015): 362-371. https://www.sciencedirect.com/science/article/pii/S0016718515001037

Klotz, Robert J. *The Politics of Internet Communication.* Lanham, MD: Rowman & Littlefield, 2004.

Leahy, Michael. *Porn University: What College Students Are Really Saying About Sex on Campus.* Chicago: Northfield Pub., 2009.

Loofbourow, Lili. "The female price of male pleasure." January 25, 2018. The Week. https://theweek.com/articles/749978/female-price-male-pleasure

Lynn, Michael, Michael C. Sturman, Christie Ganley, Elizabeth Adams, Mathew Douglas, and Jessica McNeal. "Consumer Racial Discrimination in Tipping: A Replication and Extension." 2008. The Scholarly Commons, Cornell University School of Hotel Administration. https://scholarship.sha.cornell.edu/cgi/viewcontent.cgi?referer=&httpsredir=1&article=1030&context=articles

Malito, Alessandra. "Women are about to control a massive amount of wealth but can't find anyone to manage it." MarketWatch. May 15, 2017. https://www.marketwatch.com/story/women-are-about-to-control-a-massive-amount-of-wealth-but-cant-find-anyone-to-manage-it-2017-05-12

Mazumder, Bhashkar and Sarah Miller. "The Effects of the Massachusetts Health Reform on Household Financial Distress." Federal Reserve Bank of Chicago. July 2015. https://www.chicagofed.org/~/media/publications/working-papers/2014/wp2014-01-pdf.pdf

McCall, Rosie. "What Is 'Snapchat Dysmorphia'? The Latest Plastic Surgery Trend Worrying Experts." iflscience!.com. August 6, 2018. https://www.iflscience.com/health-and-medicine/what-is-snapchat-dysmorphia-the-latest-plastic-surgery-trend-worrying-experts/page-2/

Mills, Nancy. "Plight Of Women Directors Improved--But Not Much: As Directors Guild Turns 50, Its Female Members Reassess Their Progress During the Past 6 Years." *Los Angeles Times.* November 17, 1986. http://articles.latimes.com/1986-11-17/entertainment/ca-3890_1_women-directors/2

Minarcik, Jenny, Chad T. Wetterneck, and Mary B. Short. "The effects of sexually explicit material use on romantic relationship dynamics." US National Library of Medicine, National Institutes of Health. October 26, 2016.https://www.ncbi.nlm.nih.gov/pmc/articles/PMC5370376/

Morris, Rhett and Mariana Penido. "How Did Silicon Valley Become Silicon Valley." Endeavor Insight. July 29, 2014. https://endeavor.org/research/new-endeavor-insight-report-analyzes-the-source-of-silicon-valleys-development/

Murphy, Shaunna. "Half of Film School Grads Are Women—So Why Are Only 1.9% Directing Big Budget Films?" MTV News. May 13, 2015. http://www.mtv.com/news/2159771/female-directors-college/

National Conference of State Legislators. "State Policies on Sex Education in Schools: Why Is Sexual Education Taught in Schools?" March 21, 2019. http://www.ncsl.org/research/health/state-policies-on-sex-education-in-schools.aspx

The National Susan B. Anthony Museum & House. "Her Life." http://susanbanthonyhouse.org/her-story/biography.php

Nelson, Christina, Toni Porter, and Kayla Reiman. "Examining Quality in Family Child Care: An Evaluation of All Our Kin."

2015. http://allourkin.org/sites/default/files/UserFriendly1-rev7%20%281%29.pdf

Nemy, Enid. "Muriel Siebert, a Determined Trailblazer for Women on Wall Street, Dies at 84." *New York Times.* August 25, 2013. http://www.nytimes.com/2013/08/26/business/muriel-siebert-first-woman-to-own-a-seat-on-wall-st-dies-at-80.html

Nick U. "Kelly Sue DeConnick explains the Sexy Lamp Test." YouTube video. Published March 11, 2016. https://www.youtube.com/watch?v=_TAG8Pd20DY

The Nielsen Company. "Hispanic Influence Reaches New Heights in The U.S." Nielsen Insights. August 23, 2016. http://www.nielsen.com/us/en/insights/news/2016/hispanic-influence-reaches-new-heights-in-the-us.html

Obama, Barack. "Remarks by the President at United States of Women Summit." June 14, 2016. https://obamawhitehouse.archives.gov/the-press-office/2016/06/14/remarks-president-united-states-women-summit

The Oregon History Project. "Child Service Centers, Swan Island shipyards." Last updated March 17, 2018. https://oregonhistoryproject.org/articles/child-service-centers-swan-island-shipyards/#.WeYj7tOGNs0

Piven, Frances Fox. *The Breaking of the American Social Compact.* New York: The New Press, 1998.

Quick, Miriam and Stephanie Tomasevic. "Diversity in Tech: Employee breakdown of key technology companies." 2017. http://www.informationisbeautiful.net/visualizations/diversity-in-tech/

RAINN. "Victims of Sexual Violence: Statistics." https://www.rainn.org/statistics/victims-sexual-violence

Robb, David. "EEOC: Major Studios Failed To Hire Female Directors; Lawsuit Looms." Deadline. February 15, 2017. https://

deadline.com/2017/02/hollywood-studios-female-directors-eeoc-investigation-1201912590/

Sears, Jocelyn. "Why Women Couldn't Wear Pants on the Senate Floor Until 1993." Mental Floss. March 22, 2017. http://mentalfloss.com/article/93384/why-women-couldnt-wear-pants-senate-floor-until-1993

Silicon Valley Bank. "Women in Technology Leadership 2019." *Silicon Valley Bank Women in Technology Leadership Report.* March 2019. https://www.svb.com/women-in-technology

Slaughter, Anne-Marie. "Anne-Marie Slaughter envisions an America where caring is as important as competing." September 5, 2013. *Washington Post.* https://www.washingtonpost.com/opinions/anne-marie-slaughter-envisions-an-america-where-caring-is-as-important-as-competing/2013/09/05/0cc4e726-14f5-11e3-a100-66fa8fd9a50c_story.html?utm_term=.2d8ca050b21d

Slayen, Galla. "The Scary Reality of a Real-Life Barbie Doll." Huff-Post. April 8, 2011. https://www.huffingtonpost.com/galia-slayen/the-scary-reality-of-a-re_b_845239.html

Sun, Rebecca. "Study Finds 80 Percent of Female Directors Made Only One Movie in 10 Years." *The Hollywood Reporter.* February 1, 2017. https://www.hollywoodreporter.com/news/study-finds-80-percent-female-directors-made-one-movie-10-years-970896

TEDx Talks. "The Stand for Self-Love: Amy Pence-Brown." May 2, 2016. https://www.youtube.com/watch?v=VnTLFlQ419s

United States Department of Justice. "Title IX of the Education Amendments of 1972." https://www.justice.gov/crt/title-ix-education-amendments-1972

U.S. Department of Health and Human Services, Centers for Disease Control and Prevention, National Center for Health Statistics. "Summary Health Statistics: National Health

Interview Survey, 2015." https://ftp.cdc.gov/pub/Health_ Statistics/NCHS/NHIS/SHS/2015_SHS_Table_A-15.pdf

Veghte, Ben. "NVCA Unveils Resources to Help Address Sexual Harassment in Venture Ecosystem." February 22, 2018. https://nvca.org/pressreleases_category/diversity/

Women in the World Staff. "'Original Six' who sued Hollywood studios in 1980s talk gender discrimination." March 11, 2016. https://womenintheworld.com/2016/03/11/original-six-who-sued-hollywood-studios-in-1980s-talk-gender-discrimination/

Women's Sports Foundation. "Title IX Myths and Facts." March 18, 2013. https://www.womenssportsfoundation.org/advocate/title-ix-issues/what-is-title-ix/title-ix-myths-facts/

Your Dictionary. "Muriel Siebert Facts." https://biography.yourdictionary.com/muriel-siebert

Zarya, Valentina. "Venture Capital's Funding Gender Gap Is Actually Getting Worse." Fortune. March 13, 2017. http://fortune.com/2017/03/13/female-founders-venture-capital/

Scattered throughout the book are lines of verse from some of my favorite women poets. Find out more about them here:

Angelou, Maya. "Caged Bird." *Shaker, Why Don't You Sing?* New York: Random House, 1983.

———. "Still I Rise." *And Still I Rise: A Book of Poems.* New York: Random House, 1978.

Barbauld, Anna Laetitia. "The Rights of Women." Poetry Foundation. https://www.poetryfoundation.org/poems/43615/the-rights-of-women

Browning, Elizabeth Barrett. *Aurora Leigh, First Book* (1857). Reissue edition. New York: Oxford University Press, 2008.

Button Poetry. "Brenna Twohy—'Fantastic Breasts and Where to Find Them.'" 2014. https://www.youtube.com/watch?v= bXey2_i7GOA

Clifton, Lucille. "won't you celebrate with me." *Book of Light*. Fort Worden Historical State Park, WA: Copper Canyon Press, 1993.

Diamond, Shea. "I Am Her." 2016. https://www.youtube.com/watch? v=4_zOOnvB7K8

Doshi, Tishani. "The River of Girls." Fort Worden Historical State Park, WA: Copper Canyon Press, 2013.

Finch, Countess of Winchilsea Anne. "The Introduction." 1713. *The Poems of Anne, Countess of Winchilsea*. Chicago: University of Chicago Press, 1903.

Gill, Nikita. "Fire." *Wild Embers: Poems of Rebellion, Fire and Beauty*. New York: Hachette Books, 2017.

Greyhaus, Jessica. "Imani Cezanne Heels." Poem Hunter. 2019. https://www.poemhunter.com/poem/imani-cezanne-heels/

Johnson, Georgia Douglas. "The Heart of a Woman." *The Heart of a Woman and Other Poems*. The Cornhill Company, 1918.

Jordan, June. "Poem About My Rights." *Directed by Desire: The Collected Poems of June Jordan*. Fort Worden Historical State Park, WA: Copper Canyon Press, 2005.

Kizer, Carolyn. "Semele Recycled." *Cool, Calm & Collected*. Fort Worden Historical State Park, WA: Copper Canyon Press, 2002.

Loy, Mina. "Parturition." Poetry Foundation. https://www.poetry foundation.org/poems/145363/parturition

Lorde, Audre. "Power." *The Collected Poems of Audre Lorde*. New York: W. W. Norton and Company Inc., 1978.

——. "A Woman Speaks." *The Collected Poems of Audre Lorde*. New York: W. W. Norton & Company, Inc., 1997.

——. "Who Said It Was Simple." *From a Land Where Other People Live*. Detroit, MI: Broadside Press, 1973.

Morgan, Robin. "Matrilineal Descent." *Monster.* New York: Random House, Inc., 1972.

Plath, Sylvia. "Lady Lazarus." *Collected Poems.* New York: Harper-Collins Publishers, 1992.

Rossetti, Christina. "Goblin Market." Poetry Foundation. https://www.poetryfoundation.org/poems/44996/goblin-market

Rukeyser, Muriel. "Käthe Kollwitz." *The Collected Poems of Muriel Rukeyser.* Pittsburgh, PA: University of Pittsburgh Press, 2006.

——. "The Speed of Darkness." *The Collected Poems of Muriel Rukeyser.* Evanston, IL: TriQuarterly Books, 1992.

Sexton, Anne. "Her Kind." *The Complete Poems by Anne Sexton.* New York: Houghton Mifflin Company, 1981.

Shaughnessy, Brenda. "Postfeminism." *Interior with Sudden Joy.* New York: Farrar, Straus and Giroux, 1999.

Shire, Warsan. "For Women Who Are 'Difficult' to Love." https://www.mic.com/articles/141711/here-s-the-warsan-shire-poem-that-caught-beyonc-s-attention-for-lemonade

Stoddard, Elizabeth Drew Barstow. "Nameless Pain." *She Wields a Pen: American Women Poets of the Nineteenth Century.* Iowa City, IA: University of Iowa Press, 1997.

Studdard, Melissa. "Respect." Originally published in Poem-a-Day on July 24, 2015, by the Academy of American Poets. https://poets.org/poem/respect

Swenson, May. "Women." *New and Selected Things Taking Place.* New York: Little Brown, 1978.

TED. "Sarah. Kay:'B' (If I Should Have a Daughter).'" TED2011. https://www.ted.com/talks/sarah_kay_if_i_should_have_a_daughter/transcript?language=en

At the time of writing, all the URL, publication information, and statistics are current. Please note that over time, information and/or access to certain pages may change.

Index

Acknowledgments

"The only people with whom you should try to get even are those who have helped you."

To everyone who agreed to be featured in this work: I am incredibly grateful for your time and your contribution to making the workplace, and the world, better for women. We need to cultivate many, many more of you. And everyone who granted me an interview, gave of their time, and contributed generously to this work: you helped fill in the stories and the framing, none of which I could have built without you.

Ana Arriola
Alyza Bohbot
Sheri Byrne-Haber
Tracy Chadwell
June Choi
Bob Dorf
Ronan Dunne
Rand Fishkin
Cindy Gallop
Maria Giese

Kat Gordon
Arlan Hamilton
AJ Jacobs
Susie Jaramillo
Arnita Johnson
Susan Kimberlin
Jody Lauren Miller
Laura Okmin
Amy Pence-Brown
Dr. Amy Person

Angel Rich
Kerry Robinson
Jessica Sager
Lauren Tilghman
Lauren Tilstra
Lo Toney
Janna Wagner
Cheri Wenger

To my early readers, Daisy Abreu, Richard Fouts, and Kathy Pfeiffer, who provided invaluable advice and direction: your intelligence and generosity are written into these pages. Every single page. Thank you.

To Jenn Grace, the most patient, kind, and reasonable publisher in the world, and her talented team at PYP.

To the women who lifted me up throughout my career: each of you has inspired this work. Without your encouragement, your sponsorship, your generosity, and example, I'd have learned nothing to inform these pages. Linda Peters, Susan Vickers, Joyce Fubini, Regina Paolillo, Melissa Brunetti, Ann Laffaye, Ann Yang, Lynn Sechrest, Laura Ramos, Susan McPherson, Elaine Walsh, and Lin Whaley (twice!).

To my beloved angels who lifted me during our shared time on this earth and are still, somehow, giving me great advice: Andrew, Mary Ann Wasil, Diana Cirillo, and Mary Loh.

To Captain Ridiculous, my spiritual advisor.

To the dear friends who tirelessly listened to me talk about this, who kept my coffee mug, my whiskey and wine glasses full, who encouraged me, who kept me laughing, and kept me from quitting: Richard, Daisy, Kathy, Sharon, Moira, Melissa, Aine, Abir, Audrey, Tobi, Miles, Peter, Steve, PJ, Travs, Rodney, Gina, Janis, beautiful Emily, my extended family at the Irish Business Organization of New York, and Danielle, John, Geoff, and everyone at 116 Crown.

This book would not have been possible without the years of unconditional love, support, and generosity from my family. As an adoptee, I am keenly aware that everything good in my life is only possible through a few incredible moments that collided, giving me my parents, my brother, my sister-in-law and my nephews. I am truly luckier than I deserve, and it is the coordination of these otherwise random events that confirms for me the existence of a benevolent god.

About the Author

Eileen Scully is an international keynote speaker and founder and CEO of The Rising Tides, a consulting firm that makes the workplace better for women through assessment and advisory services.

She is a SheSource Expert with the Women's Media Center and has been interviewed by *Forbes*, the *Boston Globe*, Standard and Poor's Global Market Intelligence, Thrive Global, *Psychology Today*, and *Inc*.

In December of 2018, Eileen was named to *Irish America Magazine*'s 2018 Business 100 list, the second consecutive year she received this prestigious and deeply meaningful honor. *Irish Echo* named Eileen one of their Community Champions in April of 2019.

In June of 2016, she was one of 5,000 global advocates for women and girls invited by the Obama White House to participate in the United State of Women. In April of 2017, she spoke at the first ever Diversity in Marketing and Advertising Summit in London— the only event of its kind focused on fostering greater diversity and inclusion in the industry. In August of 2018, Eileen spoke at the first Women In Engineering conference sponsored by the global Institute of Electrical and Electronics Engineers in Tunisia.

In September of 2018, she delivered her first TED talk, "How Women Can Succeed in a World Built Without Them," at the TEDx conference in Sfax, Tunisia.

In November of 2018, The Rising Tides launched the Leadership Diversity Index, the first comprehensive measurement of the representation of women and people of color on corporate boards of directors and executive leadership teams.

She serves as a founding committee member on the Women's Networking Initiative for the Irish Business Organization of New York. She is a past Chair and former Board Member of the Get in Touch Foundation and former advisor to the Innovadores Foundation. In her spare time, she volunteers as an event photographer for Special Olympics Connecticut and Integrated Refugee and Immigrant Services (IRIS).

She lives on the East Coast, never far from the ocean, with her ridiculous Basset Hound, Beukeboom.

CPSIA information can be obtained
at www.ICGtesting.com
Printed in the USA
LVHW071138110919
630691LV00036B/277/P

9 781946 384720